ask me another

A Book of Literary Quizzes

ask me another

A Book of Literary Quizzes

by George S. Phyllides

Dover Publications, Inc., New York

Published in Canada by General Publishing Company, Ltd.,
30 Lesmill Road, Don Mills, Toronto, Ontario.
Published in the United Kingdom by Constable and Company, Ltd.,
10 Orange Street, London WC 2.

Ask Me Another: A Book of Literary Quizzes is a new work,
first published by Dover Publications, Inc., in 1970.

Standard Book Number: 486-22321-3
Library of Congress Catalog Card Number: 69–19729

Manufactured in the United States of America
Dover Publications, Inc.
180 Varick Street
New York, N.Y. 10014

contents

		QUESTIONS	ANSWERS
Part I: Freedom of Choice			
1.	Biographical Matters	PAGE 1	PAGE 117
2.	Shakespeare	2	117
3.	Greeks and Romans	3	117
4.	Animals and Nature	4	118
5.	Pseudonyms	5	118
6.	Omnibuses	6	118
7.	Which Novel?	8	118
8.	Poetry	9	118
9.	What's It About?	10	119
10.	Protagonists	11	119
11.	Dramatis Personae	13	119
12.	The Children's Bookshelf	14	119
13.	Interesting Locales	15	120
14.	The Game of Authors	16	120
15.	Mythology	17	120
16.	Occupations	19	120
17.	Models, Prototypes and Alter Egos	20	120
18.	Crime and Punishment	21	121
19.	Grab-bag	22	121
20.	The World We Live In	24	121
21.	Friends and Lovers	25	121
22.	Wars and Weapons	26	121
23.	Kinship	27	122
24.	Literary Terms	29	122
25.	Religion and Philosophy	30	122
26.	Where Are We?	31	122
27.	Novels	32	122
28.	Guess the Author	34	123

29.	The Theatre	PAGE 35	PAGE 123
30.	Main Characters	36	123
31.	Supporting Figures	37	123
32.	It's All Relative	39	123
33.	Science Fiction and the Unknown	40	124
34.	Places	41	124
35.	Literary Style	42	124
36.	Disasters	43	124
37.	Miscellaneous Writers	44	124
38.	Myths and Legends	46	125
39.	Drama	47	125
40.	Poets	48	125
41.	Who Wrote . . . ?	49	125
42.	Leading Figures	50	125
43.	Settings	51	126
44.	Professions	53	126
45.	Shorter Works	54	126
46.	Characters in the Novel	55	126
47.	Adventure	56	126
48.	Non-fiction	58	127
49.	Husbands and Wives	59	127

Part II: Compatibility

1.	The Animal Kingdom	61	129
2.	Fictional Detectives	62	129
3.	Machinations	62	129
4.	Utopias	62	130
5.	For the Birds	63	130
6.	Personae	63	130
7.	People and Places	63	130
8.	Locale	64	130
9.	Part of the Whole	64	131
10.	Have a Heart	65	131
11.	Divine Romans	65	131
12.	Heaven and Hell	65	131
13.	Italian Literature	66	131
14.	Who's Who	66	132
15.	The Older Generation	66	132
16.	Epistolary Literature	67	132
17.	Home Sweet Home	67	132

	PAGE 67	PAGE 132
18. Mothers	PAGE 67	PAGE 132
19. Doctors and Medicine	68	133
20. Nominal Titles	68	133
21. Mot Juste	68	133
22. Military and Naval	69	133
23. Picaresque Novels	69	133
24. Be It Ever So Humble	69	134
25. The World of Henry James	70	134
26. All That Glitters	70	134
27. "Black"	70	134
28. Scene of Action	71	134
29. A Collection	71	135
30. Biography and Autobiography	71	135
31. Mirabile Dictu	71	135
32. Brevity	72	135
33. Of Ships	72	135
34. Itinerary	72	136
35. Essays Famous and Popular	73	136
36. North, East, South, West	73	136
37. Literary Terms	73	136
38. The Time Has Come	74	136
39. Flowers	75	137
40. The B's Have It	75	137
41. Epic	75	137
42. Bride and Bridegroom	76	137
43. His Infernal Majesty	76	137
44. First Person Singular	76	138
45. Palette and Brush	77	138
46. Personal Pronoun "You"	77	138
47. Mr., Mrs. and Miss	77	138
48. Strange Titles	78	138
49. American Novels	78	139
50. Worlds	78	139
51. To Sleep	79	139
52. Months	79	139
53. Tempus Fugit	79	139
54. Biographies	80	140
55. Man and God	80	140
56. Money! Money! Money!	81	140
57. Summum Bonum	81	140
58. Daily Pursuits	81	140
59. Autobiographies	81	141
60. Bilingual Olympians	82	141

61. Literary Span   PAGE 82   PAGE 141
62. Address Unknown   82   141
63. From Book to Stage   83   141
64. Omega   83   142
65. Essays   84   142
66. Crenelations   84   142
67. In Vino Veritas   84   142
68. Fictional Teachers   85   142
69. Where the Heart Is   85   143
70. Shaviana   86   143

Part III: Creeping Ellipsis

 1. One, Two, Three   87   145
 2. Complete the Title   87   145
 3. Russian Literature   88   145
 4. Shakespearean Heroines   88   146
 5. The Grim Reaper   88   146
 6. Famous First Lines   89   146
 7. Real People in Fiction   89   146
 8. Complete the Pair   89   146
 9. The World of Dickens   90   147
10. Missing Names   90   147
11. One or the Other   90   147
12. Famous Sonnets   90   147
13. Flights of Poetry   91   147
14. Children in Fiction   91   148
15. Royalty and Nobility   91   148
16. Name the Poem   91   148
17. Women in Poetry   92   148
18. Triple Threat   92   148
19. Fictional Pairs   92   149
20. Missing Names   93   149
21. Literary "Props"   93   149
22. God and Man   93   149
23. Identity   94   149
24. A Writer and His Lady   94   150
25. Young Heroes   94   150
26. American Plays   94   150
27. First and Last   94   150
28. Memoirs, Biographies and Autobiographies   95   150

29.	The E's Have It	PAGE 95	PAGE 151
30.	Books in Series	95	151
31.	Poetry in Flower	96	151
32.	The Animal Kingdom	96	151
33.	Two in One	96	151
34.	Fallen Angels	96	152
35.	Lesser-known Novels of Better-known Writers	97	152
36.	Pairs as Titles	97	152
37.	Greece and Rome	97	152
38.	School or Movement	97	152
39.	Quotations	98	153
40.	First Lines	98	153
41.	Musical Terms in Titles	98	153
42.	Spectral Forms	98	153
43.	Moods and Emotions	99	153
44.	Literary Regions	99	154
45.	More Animals	99	154
46.	Names	99	154
47.	Murder Most Foul	100	154
48.	Brothers and Sisters	100	154
49.	Trilogies and Tetralogies	100	155
50.	Cherchez la Femme	100	155
51.	The Ages of Man	101	155
52.	Twentieth-century English Novels	101	155
53.	Titles from Literature	101	155
54.	Place-names	101	156
55.	What's the Weather?	102	156
56.	Mentors and Teachers	102	156
57.	"Green"	102	156
58.	Sounds Familiar	102	156
59.	Men and Women	103	157
60.	Windy Weather	103	157
61.	Good Hunting!	103	157
62.	Volumes of Poetry	103	157
63.	Member of the Family	104	157
64.	First Names	104	158
65.	Trios	104	158
66.	Men of the Cloth	104	158
67.	Shakespearean Characters	105	158
68.	Narrator or Guide	105	158
69.	To the Ladies	105	159
70.	Same Initials	105	159

71.	Star-crossed Lovers	PAGE 106	PAGE 159
72.	Background of War	106	159
73.	Room for All	106	159
74.	Adventures or Adventurers	106	160
75.	Money! Money! Money!	107	160
76.	Alliterative Titles	107	160
77.	Big and Little	107	160
78.	"White"	107	160
79.	Parents and Sons	108	161
80.	Fictional Children	108	161
81.	Memoirs	108	161
82.	"Gray"	108	161
83.	What's in a Name?	109	161
84.	Epithets	109	162
85.	Caesar, Antony and Cleopatra	109	162
86.	Twosome	109	162
87.	Decline and Fall	109	162
88.	The World of Dickens	110	162
89.	Greek Mythology	110	163
90.	Ménages à Trois	110	163
91.	Locus	110	163
92.	Doctors	111	163
93.	In the Family	111	163
94.	Many Moons	111	164
95.	First Person Possessive	112	164
96.	All Kinds of Men	112	164
97.	Peter, Peter	112	164
98.	Clothes Make the Man	112	164
99.	"Red"	112	165
100.	The Children's Corner	113	165
101.	The Four Seasons	113	165
102.	Trios	113	165
103.	Siblings	113	165
104.	Children to the Fore	114	166
105.	Same Titles, Different Authors	114	166
106.	Place-names	114	166
107.	Astronomical	115	166
108.	M.D.'s and Others	115	166
109.	Trios	115	167
110.	Titular Locations	116	167
111.	Mystery and Mysteries	116	167
112.	Theatre of War	116	167
113.	Behind the Mask	116	167

ask me another

A Book of Literary Quizzes

part one

Freedom of Choice

1. Biographical Matters

1. *The Prairie Years* is part of Carl Sandburg's biography of
[A] Robert Frost   [B] John Steinbeck   [C] Robert E. Lee
[D] Abraham Lincoln   [E] Oliver Wendell Holmes

2. The novel *Young Man with a Horn* by Dorothy Baker is
based on the life of
[A] Roland   [B] Bix Beiderbecke   [C] Louis Armstrong
[D] Al Hirt   [E] Harry James

3. Virginia Woolf's *Flush* is a biography of
[A] a boy   [B] an orphan   [C] a cat   [D] a dog   [E] a horse

4. *Comédien et Martyr* is the subtitle of Jean-Paul Sartre's
critical biography of
[A] Jean Anouilh   [B] Eugène Ionesco   [C] Jean Genet
[D] Jean Giraudoux   [E] Samuel Beckett

5. *Yankee from Olympus* by Catherine Drinker Bowen is the
biography of
[A] Oliver Wendell Holmes   [B] Thomas Jefferson
[C] Francis Bacon   [D] Isaac Newton   [E] Matthew Arnold

I

6. *R.V.R.* by Hendrik van Loon is the biography of
   [A] Auguste Rodin   [B] Pierre Renoir   [C] Rembrandt
   [D] Karel Čapek   [E] François Rabelais

7. Hesketh Pearson wrote
   [A] *Abraham Lincoln*   [B] *H. L. Mencken*   [C] *Robert E. Lee*
   [D] *Oscar Wilde*   [E] *Lust for Life*

8. André Maurois' biography *Ariel* is about
   [A] Victor Hugo   [B] John Keats   [C] Lord Byron
   [D] Percy Bysshe Shelley   [E] Charles Baudelaire

9. Sheila Graham's book *Beloved Infidel* is about
   [A] William Faulkner   [B] Ernest Hemingway
   [C] John Dos Passos   [D] F. Scott Fitzgerald
   [E] Theodore Dreiser

10. *The Years with Ross* is James Thurber's biography of
    [A] a novelist   [B] an actor   [C] a poet   [D] an editor
    [E] a professor

2. Shakespeare

1. The Forest of Arden is found in
   [A] *Twelfth Night*   [B] *Cymbeline*   [C] *As You Like It*
   [D] *A Comedy of Errors*   [E] *The Tempest*

2. The man who tames the Shrew is
   [A] Orlando   [B] Bassanio   [C] Prospero   [D] Banquo
   [E] Petruchio

3. The Moor of Venice is
   [A] Shylock   [B] Polonius   [C] Banquo   [D] Othello
   [E] Prospero

4. Birnam Wood appears in
   [A] *Hamlet*   [B] *King Lear*   [C] *Macbeth*   [D] *Othello*
   [E] *Coriolanus*

5. Mark Antony's funeral oration is found in the play
   [A] *King Lear*   [B] *Antony and Cleopatra*   [C] *Hamlet*
   [D] *Macbeth*   [E] *Julius Caesar*

6. The Queen of the Amazons who appears in *A Midsummer Night's Dream* is
   [A] Atalanta   [B] Hippolyta   [C] Circe   [D] Cassandra
   [E] Daphne

7. "Age cannot wither her, nor custom stale/Her infinite variety" is Enobarbus's description of
   [A] Cordelia   [B] Calpurnia   [C] Ophelia   [D] Cleopatra
   [E] Cymbeline

8. The father of Lavinia is
   [A] Malvolio   [B] Polonius   [C] Macduff
   [D] Titus Andronicus   [E] Publius

9. Banquo's ghost appears in
   [A] *Hamlet*   [B] *Pericles*   [C] *Macbeth*
   [D] *Titus Andronicus*   [E] *Richard III*

10. In *Twelfth Night* the steward of Olivia is
    [A] Laertes   [B] Duncan   [C] Cassius   [D] Malvolio
    [E] Prospero

3. Greeks and Romans

1. The Muse of love poetry is
   [A] Clio   [B] Thalia   [C] Erato   [D] Urania   [E] Melpomene

2. The author of the first pastorals was the Greek poet
   [A] Theocritus   [B] Pindar   [C] Hesiod   [D] Homer
   [E] Aesop

3. Prometheus stole
   [A] the golden apple   [B] the shield of Achilles
   [C] the golden fleece   [D] fire from heaven
   [E] the Midas touch

4. The Satyrs were
   [A] nymphs   [B] centaurs   [C] Fates   [D] Graces
   [E] goat-men

5. The Greek god of music and poetry is
   [A] Hermes   [B] Poseidon   [C] Apollo   [D] Zeus
   [E] Hephestus

6. Juvenal was the author of
   [A] the *Satyricon*   [B] the *Golden Ass*
   [C] the *Metamorphoses*   [D] eclogues   [E] satires

7. The terms terror, pity and catharsis are associated with
   [A] Plato   [B] Epicurus   [C] Socrates   [D] Aristotle
   [E] Theocritus

8. Plato's *Symposium* is
   [A] on justice   [B] on the ideal state   [C] on love
   [D] about Socrates' trial   [E] about Socrates' death

9. The *Lives of the Twelve Caesars* was written by
   [A] Tacitus   [B] Petronius Arbiter   [C] Suetonius
   [D] Josephus   [E] Livy

10. Aeschylus wrote
    [A] *The Trojan Women*   [B] *The Frogs*   [C] *Antigone*
    [D] the *Anabasis*   [E] the Oresteia trilogy

4. Animals and Nature

1. Winnie the Pooh is a
   [A] Chinese maiden   [B] race horse   [C] teddy bear
   [D] dog   [E] cat

2. The three-headed dog of Hades was
   [A] Centaur   [B] Hydra   [C] Cerberus   [D] Minotaur
   [E] Styx

3. The animal described in *A Ring of Bright Water* by Gavin Maxwell is
[A] a swan   [B] an opossum   [C] an otter   [D] a fish
[E] a deer

4. In *Metamorphosis* by Franz Kafka, a character is transformed into
[A] a dog   [B] a horse   [C] an insect   [D] a bird   [E] a boar

5. A parrot appears in the book
[A] *The Wind in the Willows*   [B] *The Wizard of Oz*
[C] *The Sea Around Us*   [D] *The Voyages of Dr. Dolittle*
[E] *The Prince and the Pauper*

6. The name of Ulysses' dog is
[A] Pegasus   [B] Asta   [C] Nana   [D] Argus   [E] Cerberus

7. The phrase "to cultivate your garden" is found in
[A] *Steppenwolf*   [B] *Candide*   [C] *Émile*
[D] *Les Misérables*   [E] "The Necklace"

8. *The Yearling* is a novel about a lonely boy and a
[A] dog   [B] cat   [C] horse   [D] fawn   [E] cub

9. Rosinante is the horse of
[A] Agamemnon   [B] Lancelot   [C] Don Quixote
[D] Robin Hood   [E] Roland

10. Rima, the bird-girl, appears in the novel
[A] *Jane Eyre*   [B] *The Return of the Native*
[C] *The Mill on the Floss*   [D] *Green Mansions*
[E] *The Purple Land*

5. Pseudonyms

1. Another title for W. S. Maugham's *Rain* is
[A] *Ethan Frome*   [B] *Mrs. Miniver*
[C] *Miss Sadie Thompson*   [D] *Camille*   [E] *Cakes and Ale*

2. Corno di Bassetto was a pen name used by
   [A] Oscar Wilde   [B] Max Beerbohm   [C] G. B. Shaw
   [D] A. W. Pinero   [E] George Eliot

3. Abraham Van Brunt is better known as
   [A] Ichabod Crane   [B] Rip Van Winkle
   [C] Tom Sawyer   [D] Brom Bones   [E] Natty Bumppo

4. Bab was a pen name used by
   [A] Lewis Carroll   [B] Dorothy Parker   [C] Ogden Nash
   [D] Max Beerbohm   [E] W. S. Gilbert

5. The pen name of Mrs. Montagu Barstow is
   [A] Ouida   [B] Baroness Orczy   [C] George Eliot
   [D] Agatha Christie   [E] Helen MacInnes

6. Marguerite Gauthier is better known as
   [A] Nana   [B] Camille   [C] Roxane   [D] Gigi   [E] Emma

7. Jean Valjean was also known as
   [A] Javert   [B] Quasimodo   [C] Rastignac
   [D] Father Madeleine   [E] Julien Sorel

8. Little Lord Fauntleroy was
   [A] Penrod   [B] Holden Caulfield   [C] Cedric Errol
   [D] Tom Tulliver   [E] Pendennis

9. The Black Knight in *Ivanhoe* by Sir Walter Scott is
   [A] Quentin Durward   [B] Cedric   [C] Athelstane
   [D] Richard the Lionhearted   [E] Kenilworth

10. The pen name of Eric Hugh Blair is
    [A] Saki   [B] Elia   [C] George Orwell   [D] O. Henry
    [E] Samuel Clemens

6. Omnibuses

1. *Molloy* and *Malone Dies* are parts of a trilogy by
   [A] John Braine   [B] Albert Camus   [C] John Updike
   [D] Upton Sinclair   [E] Samuel Beckett

2. *Swann's Way* is the first volume of the series called
   [A] *The Human Comedy*   [B] *U.S.A.*
   [C] *Remembrance of Things Past*   [D] *Les Thibault*
   [E] *Joseph and His Brothers*

3. *Burnt Norton* is part of
   [A] *The Waste Land*   [B] *Four Quartets*   [C] *Idylls of the King*
   [D] *The Age of Anxiety*   [E] *A Shropshire Lad*

4. The first five books of the Bible are called
   [A] The Beatitudes   [B] The Analects   [C] The Koran
   [D] The Pentateuch   [E] The Meditations

5. The story of Susanna and the Elders is found in
   [A] The Koran   [B] The New Testament   [C] The Apocrypha
   [D] *The Divine Comedy*   [E] *Paradise Lost*

6. The author of the trilogy *House of Earth* is
   [A] John Steinbeck   [B] Knut Hamsun   [C] Pearl Buck
   [D] Edith Wharton   [E] Eudora Welty

7. The author of *Spoon River Anthology* is
   [A] Vachel Lindsay   [B] E. A. Robinson
   [C] Edgar Allan Poe   [D] Hart Crane
   [E] Edgar Lee Masters

8. The epic that is a sequel to the story of the siege of Troy is
   [A] the *Iliad*   [B] *The Divine Comedy*   [C] the *Odyssey*
   [D] the *Anabasis*   [E] the *Satyricon*

9. The last volume of the *Studs Lonigan Trilogy* by James T.
   Farrell is entitled
   [A] *In Dubious Battle*   [B] *Of Time and the River*
   [C] *Judgment Day*   [D] *The Past Recaptured*   [E] *Clea*

10. *Father Goriot* by Balzac is one of the volumes in the series
    [A] *U.S.A.*   [B] *Remembrance of Things Past*
    [C] *The Human Comedy*   [D] *Les Thibault*
    [E] *Rougon-Macquart*

7. Which Novel?

1. The novel that deals with the fate of Hitler refugees in Paris is
   [A] *The Disenchanted*   [B] *In Dubious Battle*
   [C] *Arch of Triumph*   [D] *The Big Sky*
   [E] *Strangers and Brothers*

2. Daphne du Maurier is the author of
   [A] *Memento Mori*   [B] *Women in Love*   [C] *The Scapegoat*
   [D] *The Group*   [E] *A Severed Head*

3. Shirley Jackson wrote
   [A] *Delta Wedding*   [B] *The Castle*   [C] *The Centaur*
   [D] *We Have Always Lived in the Castle*   [E] *The Unicorn*

4. Romain Gary is the author of
   [A] *The Stranger*   [B] *The Leopard*   [C] *The Pledge*
   [D] *Roots of Heaven*   [E] *Strait Is the Gate*

5. Kingsley Amis' novel about a college instructor is
   [A] *The Groves of Academe*   [B] *The Browning Version*
   [C] *Lord Jim*   [D] *Lucky Jim*   [E] *The Contenders*

6. Lafcadio Hearn wrote
   [A] *The Lion*   [B] *Tale of Genji*   [C] *Some Prefer Nettles*
   [D] *Youma*   [E] *The Mask*

7. Anthony Trollope is the author of
   [A] *Adam Bede*   [B] *Pendennis*   [C] *Barchester Towers*
   [D] *Our Mutual Friend*   [E] *Villette*

8. T. L. Peacock wrote
   [A] *The Castle*   [B] *The Castle of Otranto*   [C] *Crotchet Castle*
   [D] *The Court and the Castle*   [E] *Castle Rackrent*

9. The novel for which Edith Wharton was awarded the Pulitzer prize is
   [A] *The House of Mirth*   [B] *The Custom of the Country*
   [C] *The Age of Innocence*   [D] *The Buccaneers*
   [E] *The Old Maid*

10. William Styron is the author of
    [A] *The Centaur* [B] *The Ponder Heart*
    [C] *Lie Down in Darkness* [D] *The Middle of the Journey*
    [E] *The Group*

8. Poetry

1. The Whitman poem inspired by Lincoln's death is
   [A] "Death, Be Not Proud" [B] "O Captain! My Captain!"
   [C] "The Soldier" [D] "I Have a Rendezvous With Death"
   [E] "Barbara Frietchie"

2. Chaucer translated from the French
   [A] *Song of Roland* [B] *Romance of the Rose*
   [C] *Heptaméron* [D] Ronsard's poems [E] Villon's poems

3. The albatross appears in the poem
   [A] "The Raven" [B] "The Hound of Heaven"
   [C] "Ode to a Skylark"
   [D] "The Rime of the Ancient Mariner"
   [E] "Ode to the West Wind"

4. The "forest primeval" is found in the poem
   [A] *Hiawatha* [B] "A Psalm of Life" [C] *Evangeline*
   [D] "Invictus" [E] "The Hollow Men"

5. The English poet who poisoned himself is
   [A] Alexander Pope [B] Thomas Gray
   [C] Percy Bysshe Shelley [D] Thomas Chatterton
   [E] William Morris

6. The lyric "Loveliest of Trees" by Housman is from the collection called
   [A] *Flowers of Evil* [B] *Leaves of Grass*
   [C] *A Shropshire Lad* [D] *The Waste Land*
   [E] *The Seasons*

7. Elizabeth B. Browning wrote a novel in blank verse entitled
[A] *Idylls of the King*   [B] *The Lady of the Lake*
[C] *Aurora Leigh*   [D] *The Defence of Guenevere*
[E] *John Brown's Body*

8. "The World Is Too Much with Us" by William Wordsworth is
[A] an ode   [B] verse drama   [C] a pastoral   [D] a sonnet
[E] an idyll

9. Robert Frost's first volume of poetry was
[A] *In the Clearing*   [B] *A Boy's Will*   [C] *North of Boston*
[D] *West-Running Brook*   [E] *A Masque of Mercy*

10. William Cullen Bryant's poem "Thanatopsis" is about
[A] youth   [B] joy   [C] success   [D] death   [E] ambition

9. What's It About?

1. George Orwell's *Animal Farm* is an allegory about
[A] love   [B] scholasticism   [C] the church
[D] communism   [E] pastoral poetry

2. *Lie Down in Darkness* by William Styron is a novel about
[A] a demagogue   [B] the American Revolution
[C] an architect   [D] the disintegration of a family
[E] the country-club set

3. In *The Ambassadors* by Henry James, Lambert Strether is sent to Europe
[A] to study   [B] to travel
[C] to marry Madame de Vionnet
[D] to bring home Chad Newsome   [E] to paint

4. *The Thirty-Nine Steps* by John Buchan is about
[A] a long journey   [B] a haunted castle
[C] an international plot   [D] the ascent of a mountain
[E] a religious conversion

5. The theme of *The Devil and Daniel Webster* by Stephen Vincent Benét is
   [A] Freudian   [B] Faustian   [C] picaresque   [D] idyllic
   [E] chivalric

6. *The Forty Days of Musa Dagh* by Franz Werfel is a novel about
   [A] Greeks vs. Romans   [B] Danes vs. Germans
   [C] French vs. British   [D] Armenians vs. Turks
   [E] Italians vs. Russians

7. Rousseau's novel *Émile* is
   [A] a love story   [B] a pastoral romance   [C] a gothic tale
   [D] a treatise on education   [E] a classical drama

8. *Hercules, My Shipmate* by Robert Graves is about
   [A] the Sphinx   [B] the labors of Hercules
   [C] the Argonauts and the Golden Fleece
   [D] the descent to Hades   [E] the Trojan War

9. Thomas De Quincey's *Confessions* are about
   [A] crimes   [B] sins   [C] youthful follies
   [D] drug addiction   [E] literary pursuits

10. *The Octopus* by Frank Norris is a novel about
    [A] the fishing industry   [B] the wheat market
    [C] fruit-growers   [D] ranchers against the railroad
    [E] factory workers

10. Protagonists

1. The hero of *Room at the Top* by John Braine is
   [A] Gulley Jimson   [B] Mountolive   [C] Joe Lampton
   [D] Major Scobie   [E] Stephen Hero

2. The narrator in *Moby Dick* by Herman Melville is called
   [A] Isaac   [B] Israfel   [C] Ishmael   [D] Ichabod   [E] Ivan

3. Deirdre is a heroine of
   [A] Norse mythology   [B] Arthurian legends
   [C] Irish legend   [D] Roman mythology
   [E] the Arabian Nights

4. Peter Quint appears in
   [A] *Sons and Lovers*   [B] *Vanity Fair*
   [C] *The Turn of the Screw*   [D] *Brighton Rock*
   [E] *The Foxglove Saga*

5. André Gide's "Immoralist" is
   [A] Lafcadio   [B] Bernard   [C] Michel   [D] Jérôme
   [E] Olivier

6. The hero of *The Red and the Black* by Stendhal is
   [A] Rawdon Crawley   [B] Jake Barnes   [C] Julien Sorel
   [D] Frédéric Moreau   [E] Inspector Maigret

7. Henry Fleming is a soldier in
   [A] *A Farewell to Arms*   [B] *Three Soldiers*
   [C] *The Young Lions*   [D] *The Red Badge of Courage*
   [E] *From Here to Eternity*

8. Isabel, Milly, Catherine, Maisie are heroines in the novels of
   [A] George Meredith   [B] Iris Murdoch   [C] Henry James
   [D] D. H. Lawrence   [E] Mary McCarthy

9. Carol Kennicott is the heroine of
   [A] *The Sun Also Rises*   [B] *The Sound and the Fury*
   [C] *Main Street*   [D] *Tobacco Road*   [E] *Ten North Frederick*

10. The man who became the Count of Monte Cristo is
    [A] Armand Duval   [B] Candide   [C] Edmond Dantès
    [D] Jean Valjean   [E] Javert

11. Dramatis Personae

1. Lady Bracknell is a character in Oscar Wilde's
   [A] *The Picture of Dorian Gray*
   [B] *The Importance of Being Earnest*
   [C] *An Ideal Husband*   [D] *Lord Savile's Crime*   [E] *Salome*

2. Fawley is the surname of
   [A] *Lord Jim*   [B] *Jude the Obscure*
   [C] *The Prisoner of Zenda*   [D] *Frankenstein*
   [E] *Moby Dick*

3. A man called K. appears in
   [A] *Metamorphosis*   [B] *Doctor Faustus*   [C] *The Castle*
   [D] *The Possessed*   [E] *Steppenwolf*

4. The creator of Harry the Horse was
   [A] Ring Lardner   [B] O. Henry   [C] Damon Runyon
   [D] Henry Miller   [E] Erskine Caldwell

5. A character who appears in *Light in August* by William
   Faulkner is
   [A] Popeye   [B] Jeeter Lester   [C] Joe Christmas
   [D] George Babbitt   [E] Eugene Gant

6. Clélia helps Fabrizio to escape in
   [A] *The Red and the Black*   [B] *Les Misérables*
   [C] *Germinal*   [D] *Colomba*   [E] *The Charterhouse of Parma*

7. Thursday and Friday are characters created respectively by
   [A] Charles Dickens and Evelyn Waugh
   [B] W. M. Thackeray and George Eliot
   [C] Daniel Defoe and Jonathan Swift
   [D] G. K. Chesterton and Daniel Defoe
   [E] R. L. Stevenson and James F. Cooper

8. Noah Ackerman and Michael Whitacre are American soldiers in
[A] *The Naked and the Dead*   [B] *A Bell for Adano*
[C] *The Young Lions*   [D] *From Here to Eternity*
[E] *The Manchurian Candidate*

9. Mathilde de la Mole is a character in Stendhal's
[A] *Nana*   [B] *Thaïs*   [C] *Madame Bovary*
[D] *The Red and the Black*   [E] *The Magic Skin*

10. The man who wins the Robe in Lloyd C. Douglas' novel is
[A] Messala   [B] Caligula   [C] Nero   [D] Marcellus
[E] Brutus

12. The Children's Bookshelf

1. Christopher Robin is a character in
[A] *Peter Pan*   [B] *Treasure Island*   [C] *Lord of the Flies*
[D] *The House at Pooh Corner*   [E] *Bambi*

2. The children followed
[A] the Hunchback of Notre Dame   [B] Pinocchio
[C] the Pied Piper of Hamelin   [D] Ichabod Crane
[E] Simon Legree

3. Cora and Alice Munro are sisters in
[A] *Uncle Tom's Cabin*   [B] *Little Women*
[C] *The Last of the Mohicans*   [D] *Tom Sawyer*
[E] *Vanity Fair*

4. The heroine of *Peter Pan* is
[A] Rhoda Penmark   [B] Becky Sharp
[C] Wendy Darling   [D] Dorothy   [E] Lorna Doone

5. The name of the Deerslayer is
[A] Daniel Boone   [B] Natty Bumppo   [C] Ichabod Crane
[D] Clifford Pyncheon   [E] Squire Western

6. Pip is a character in
   [A] *The Mill on the Floss*   [B] *The Yearling*
   [C] *Great Expectations*   [D] *Uncle Tom's Cabin*
   [E] *Tom Sawyer*

7. Long John Silver is a character in
   [A] *Kidnapped*   [B] *Peter Pan*   [C] *Mutiny on the Bounty*
   [D] *Treasure Island*   [E] *The Hurricane*

8. Eppie brings happiness and contentment to
   [A] Uriah Heep   [B] Heathcliff   [C] Clym Yeobright
   [D] Silas Marner   [E] Rawdon Crawley

9. Brom Bones is the rival of
   [A] Tom Sawyer   [B] Holden Caulfield   [C] Penrod
   [D] Clifford Pyncheon   [E] Ichabod Crane

10. In *The Wizard of Oz*, the name of Dorothy's dog is
    [A] Nana   [B] Toto   [C] Fang   [D] Kashtanka
    [E] Argos

13. Interesting Locales

1. George Babbitt is a realtor in
   [A] Gopher Prairie   [B] Hecate County   [C] Sleepy Hollow
   [D] Zenith   [E] Libya Hill

2. In *Steppenwolf*, by Hermann Hesse, Harry Haller finds himself in
   [A] the Labyrinth   [B] Shangri-La   [C] Oceania
   [D] the Magic Theatre   [E] Nighttown

3. In *Remembrance of Things Past* Marcel meets Albertine at
   [A] Combray   [B] Balbec   [C] the Phoenix Club
   [D] Tansonville   [E] the home of Mme Verdurin

4. The third act of G. B. Shaw's *Man and Superman* is set in
   [A] Heaven   [B] Utopia   [C] Hell   [D] Purgatory
   [E] Atlantis

5. *The Return of the Native* by Thomas Hardy opens with a description of
   [A] Wessex   [B] Stonehenge   [C] Dorset
   [D] Egdon Heath   [E] Casterbridge

6. Valhalla was
   [A] a Utopia   [B] an academy
   [C] a heaven for warriors slain in battle
   [D] a Norse goddess   [E] a Norse epic

7. Candide visited a land called
   [A] Paradiso   [B] Shangri-la   [C] Eden   [D] El Dorado
   [E] Oceania

8. Penelope remained faithful to Odysseus on the island of
   [A] Lesbos   [B] Ogygia   [C] the Sirens   [D] Ithaca
   [E] Illyria

9. Lethe is the river of forgetfulness; Phlegethon is the river of
   [A] darkness   [B] bliss   [C] fire   [D] torment   [E] nymphs

10. The setting of Albert Camus' novel *The Stranger* is
    [A] Paris   [B] Amsterdam   [C] Spain   [D] North Africa
    [E] the Riviera

14. The Game of Authors

1. The author of the *Metamorphoses* is
   [A] Kafka   [B] Ovid   [C] Theocritus   [D] Horace
   [E] Juvenal

2. The author of *One Man's Meat* is
   [A] James Thurber   [B] E. B. White   [C] Robert Benchley
   [D] Evelyn Waugh   [E] Lawrence Durrell

3. The author of the novel *Amerika* is
   [A] Jean Giraudoux   [B] Thomas Mann   [C] Franz Kafka
   [D] W. S. Maugham   [E] J. D. Salinger

4. A man both author and painter is
   [A] Carl Sandburg [B] Bertrand Russell
   [C] Wallace Stevens [D] John O'Hara
   [E] Winston Churchill

5. The author of *The Infernal World of Branwell Brontë* is
   [A] Van Wyck Brooks [B] Hesketh Pearson
   [C] Daphne du Maurier [D] Irving Stone
   [E] Peter Quennell

6. The author of *Our Lady of the Flowers* is
   [A] Morris West [B] A. J. Cronin [C] Evelyn Waugh
   [D] Jean Genet [E] Aldous Huxley

7. "The Byron of Russia" was
   [A] Gogol [B] Tolstoy [C] Chekhov [D] Pushkin
   [E] Turgenev

8. The author of *The End of the Affair* is
   [A] Muriel Spark [B] Iris Murdoch [C] John Braine
   [D] Graham Greene [E] Evelyn Waugh

9. *Citizen Tom Paine* is a novel by
   [A] Kenneth Roberts [B] Thomas Costain
   [C] Howard Fast [D] Mary Renault
   [E] Margaret Mitchell

10. The author of *A Study of History* is
    [A] William Shirer [B] Frederick Allen
    [C] Bruce Catton [D] Arnold Toynbee
    [E] Claude G. Bowers

15. Mythology

1. The maid who was rescued by Perseus is
   [A] Ariadne [B] Andromeda [C] Daphne
   [D] Galatea [E] Arethusa

2. Paris awarded the Apple of Discord to
   [A] Hera   [B] Athena   [C] Artemis   [D] Aphrodite
   [E] Hestia

3. The Eumenides were the
   [A] Fates   [B] Graces   [C] Furies   [D] Muses   [E] Dryads

4. Odysseus was detained on the Isle of Ogygia by
   [A] Nausicaa   [B] Scylla   [C] Circe   [D] Calypso
   [E] Penelope

5. James Joyce's Molly is the mythological
   [A] Ariadne   [B] Andromeda   [C] Penelope   [D] Galatea
   [E] Niobe

6. Scylla and Charybdis are found in
   [A] the *Aeneid*   [B] the *Odyssey*   [C] *The Frogs*
   [D] *Robinson Crusoe*   [E] the *Iliad*

7. Antigone defied the harsh edict of
   [A] Oedipus   [B] Creon   [C] Haemon   [D] Eteocles
   [E] Polynices

8. Melpomene is the muse of
   [A] comedy   [B] love poetry   [C] narrative poetry
   [D] tragedy   [E] astronomy

9. The judge of the dead was
   [A] Cerberus   [B] Orpheus   [C] Minos   [D] Janus
   [E] Pyramus

10. *The King Must Die* and *The Bull from the Sea* by Mary
    Renault relate the adventures of
    [A] Perseus   [B] Hercules   [C] Theseus   [D] Oedipus
    [E] Orestes

16. Occupations

1. The rogue who buys up "dead souls" is called
   [A] Litvinov [B] Chichikov [C] Kirilov
   [D] Raskolnikov [E] Oblomov

2. In *The Secret Life of Walter Mitty* by James Thurber, Walter Mitty is
   [A] a criminal [B] a teacher [C] an engineer
   [D] a day dreamer [E] an architect

3. In *The Hunchback of Notre Dame* by Victor Hugo, Quasimodo is a
   [A] servant [B] circus performer [C] blacksmith
   [D] bell ringer [E] teamster

4. Livy was a Roman
   [A] poet [B] sculptor [C] historian [D] philosopher
   [E] painter

5. One of the characters in *The Heart is a Lonely Hunter* by Carson McCullers is
   [A] an elf [B] a mute [C] an evangelist [D] a spy
   [E] a sailor

6. The hero of Ayn Rand's *The Fountainhead* is
   [A] a lawyer [B] a doctor [C] an actor
   [D] an architect [E] a professor

7. Golden Boy was
   [A] an artist [B] a pilot [C] a gambler [D] a boxer
   [E] a dancer

8. Marguerite Gauthier was
   [A] a librarian [B] a maid [C] a courtesan [D] a huntress
   [E] a pioneer

9. In *Père Goriot*, by Honoré de Balzac, Madame Vauquer
   [A] writes novels   [B] has a salon
   [C] runs a boarding-house   [D] is a laundress
   [E] marries a banker

10. In *A Tale of Two Cities*, Mr. Jarvis Lorry is
    [A] a lawyer   [B] a minister   [C] a professor [D] a banker
    [E] a doctor

17. Models, Prototypes and Alter Egos

1. Sheridan Whiteside, in *The Man Who Came to Dinner*, was modeled after
   [A] Robert Benchley   [B] James Thurber
   [C] Wolcott Gibbs   [D] W. S. Gilbert
   [E] Alexander Woollcott

2. The *Iliad* and the *Odyssey* served as models for
   [A] *The Satyricon*   [B] *Marius the Epicurean*
   [C] *I, Claudius*   [D] *The Golden Ass*   [E] *The Aeneid*

3. The *Dear and Glorious Physician* of Taylor Caldwell is
   [A] Reed   [B] Albert Schweitzer   [C] St. Luke
   [D] Hippocrates   [E] Harvey

4. In *The Moon and Sixpence* by W. S. Maugham, the prototype of the hero is
   [A] Vincent Van Gogh   [B] Pablo Picasso
   [C] Claude Monet   [D] Paul Gauguin
   [E] Pierre Auguste Renoir

5. A Jane Austen novel which is a parody of the gothic novel is
   [A] *Emma*   [B] *Persuasion*   [C] *Mansfield Park*
   [D] *Northanger Abbey*   [E] *Pride and Prejudice*

6. *The Vision of Sir Launfal* by James Russell Lowell is a version of
   [A] *The Lost Weekend*   [B] the Oedipus legend
   [C] the Holy Grail legend   [D] the *Song of Roland*
   [E] the *Pilgrim's Progress*

7. In *You Can't Go Home Again* by Thomas Wolfe, Lloyd McHarg is based on the character of
   [A] Maxwell Perkins   [B] George Pierce Baker
   [C] Sinclair Lewis   [D] Upton Sinclair
   [E] Erskine Caldwell

8. Jean Cocteau's version of the Oedipus myth is entitled
   [A] *The Riddle of the Sphinx*   [B] *Oedipus Rex*
   [C] *The Infernal Machine*   [D] *Oedipus and Jocasta*
   [E] *Oedipus and Antigone*

9. Mark Rampion in *Point Counter Point* is based on the figure of Aldous Huxley's friend
   [A] Arnold Bennett   [B] Evelyn Waugh
   [C] D. H. Lawrence   [D] Bertrand Russell
   [E] T. E. Lawrence

10. Modeled on the English *Everyman*, the *Jedermann* performed at Salzburg was written by
    [A] Goethe   [B] R. M. Rilke   [C] Frank Wedekind
    [D] Hugo von Hofmannsthal   [E] Schiller

18. Crime and Punishment

1. In *The Stranger* by Albert Camus, Meursault kills
   [A] a stranger   [B] an Arab   [C] his enemy   [D] an officer
   [E] a prison guard

2. The murderer of Fyodor Karamazov is
   [A] Ivan   [B] Alyosha   [C] Smerdyakov   [D] Dimitri
   [E] Grushenka

3. The lawyer in *Dr. Jekyll and Mr. Hyde* by R. L. Stevenson is named
[A] Lanyon   [B] Utterson   [C] Trenchard
[D] Sir Danvers Carew   [E] Poole

4. A character in Franz Kafka's *The Trial* is
[A] Minos   [B] Judge Pyncheon   [C] the Advocate
[D] Judge Brack   [E] Marlow

5. In *A Passage to India* Adela Quested accuses Dr. Aziz of
[A] theft   [B] breach of promise   [C] attacking her
[D] arson   [E] disturbing the peace

6. One of the Cardinal's spies in *The Three Musketeers* by Alexandre Dumas *père* is
[A] Mme Bovary   [B] Fantine   [C] Milady
[D] Sanseverina   [E] Thérèse

7. In the *Iliad* Achilles slays
[A] Patroclus   [B] Priam   [C] Paris   [D] Menelaus
[E] Hector

8. Raskolnikov's victim in Dostoevsky's *Crime and Punishment* is
[A] a city official   [B] a lawyer   [C] a moneylender
[D] a seamstress   [E] a teacher

9. *The Crime of Sylvestre Bonnard* by Anatole France was
[A] murder   [B] grand larceny   [C] arson
[D] kidnapping   [E] embezzlement

10. The Gidean hero who commits the unmotivated act is
[A] Candide   [B] Frédéric   [C] Julien   [D] Lafcadio
[E] Meursault

19. Grab-bag

1. Bacchus was the god of
[A] speed   [B] fire   [C] the sea   [D] war   [E] wine

2. *Jean-Christophe* by Romain Rolland is the story of the life and career of
   [A] a painter [B] a musician [C] a doctor [D] a writer
   [E] a lawyer

3. Dr. Aziz' friend in *A Passage to India* by E. M. Forster is
   [A] Joe Lampton [B] Cyril Fielding [C] Basil Hallward
   [D] Mountolive [E] Lambert Strether

4. Charles Darwin wrote
   [A] *Mutiny on the Bounty* [B] *Bound East for Cardiff*
   [C] *The Voyage of the Beagle* [D] *The Caine Mutiny*
   [E] *The Innocent Voyage*

5. The Café des Deux Magots is associated with
   [A] François Rabelais [B] Molière
   [C] Jean-Paul Sartre [D] Honoré de Balzac
   [E] Eugène Ionesco

6. Arthur Koestler wrote
   [A] *The Young Caesar* [B] *Belisarius*
   [C] *The Bull from the Sea* [D] *The Gladiators*
   [E] *The Woman of Andros*

7. The daughter of Hecuba was
   [A] Helen [B] Cassandra [C] Electra [D] Antigone
   [E] Andromache

8. Altamont and Libya Hill are place names in the novels of
   [A] Sinclair Lewis [B] William Faulkner
   [C] Erskine Caldwell [D] Thomas Wolfe
   [E] Eudora Welty

9. Plautus and Terence wrote
   [A] histories [B] tragedies [C] novels [D] comedies
   [E] sonnets

10. The hypocrite in Molière's play is
    [A] Alceste [B] Harpagon [C] Tartuffe [D] Jourdain
    [E] Sganarelle

20. The World We Live In

1. Thomas Mann's story *Mario and the Magician* is about the effects of
   [A] drug addiction   [B] war on Germany   [C] occupation
   [D] Fascism in Italy   [E] unemployment

2. Vance Packard wrote
   [A] *The Exurbanites*   [B] *Red Man's America*
   [C] *The Hidden Persuaders*   [D] *Microbe Hunters*
   [E] *Language*

3. In *The Possessed* by Dostoevsky, Stavrogin is the leader of a group of
   [A] Republicans   [B] Monarchists   [C] Nihilists
   [D] Deists   [E] Humanists

4. The author of *The Culture of Cities* is
   [A] Sigfried Giedion   [B] Lewis Mumford
   [C] Howard Mumford Jones   [D] Christopher Tunnard
   [E] Vitruvius

5. The author of *Das Kapital* is
   [A] Engels   [B] Hegel   [C] Fichte   [D] Marx   [E] Lenin

6. The author of *The Social Contract* is
   [A] Marx   [B] Hegel   [C] Plato   [D] Rousseau
   [E] Carlyle

7. Henry Miller's essay on American culture is
   [A] *Tropic of Cancer*   [B] *The Colossus of Maroussi*
   [C] *The Cosmological Eye*
   [D] *The Air-Conditioned Nightmare*
   [E] *Sunday after the War*

8. A novel which brought about social legislation is
   [A] *East of Eden*   [B] *Sanctuary*   [C] *The Jungle*
   [D] *Ethan Frome*   [E] *The Yearling*

9. The expression "conspicuous waste" used by Veblen appears in the book
   [A] *The Wealth of Nations* [B] *The Affluent Society*
   [C] *The Theory of the Leisure Class*
   [D] *Religion and the Rise of Capitalism* [E] *Das Kapital*

10. Alexis de Tocqueville wrote
    [A] *The American Commonwealth*
    [B] *Democracy in America* [C] *Wealth of Nations*
    [D] *The Origin of Species* [E] *The Social Contract*

21. Friends and Lovers

1. George Moore wrote a novel about the medieval lovers
   [A] Romeo and Juliet [B] Pyramus and Thisbe
   [C] Pygmalion and Galatea [D] Héloïse and Abélard
   [E] Petrarch and Laura

2. Dorian Gray fell in love with
   [A] Eustacia Vye [B] Sibyl Vane [C] Moll Flanders
   [D] Hetty Sorrel [E] Dora Spenlow

3. Lt. Frederick Henry meets nurse Catherine Barkley in
   [A] *Three Soldiers* [B] *The Young Lions*
   [C] *A Farewell to Arms* [D] *The Naked and the Dead*
   [E] *The Enormous Room*

4. Frances Winwar's biography *The Immortal Lovers* is about
   [A] D'Annunzio and Duse [B] Thomas and Jane Carlyle
   [C] Elizabeth Barrett and Robert Browning
   [D] George Sand and Frédéric Chopin
   [E] Benjamin Constant and Mme de Staël

5. In *The Web and the Rock* by Thomas Wolfe, George Webber meets
   [A] Temple Drake [B] Roberta Alden [C] Esther Jack
   [D] Sally Bowles [E] Molly Bloom

6. In Fielding's novel, Tom Jones was steadfast in his devotion
   to
   [A] Bridget [B] Molly [C] Sophia [D] Jenny [E] Becky

7. The story of Lancelot and Elaine is found in
   [A] *The Pilgrim's Progress* [B] *Paradise Lost*
   [C] *Idylls of the King* [D] *The Deserted Village*
   [E] *The Prelude*

8. One of Emma Bovary's lovers is
   [A] Frédéric Moreau [B] Julien Sorel [C] Léon Dupuis
   [D] Armand Duval [E] Charles Grandet

9. Peter Quint's companion is
   [A] Mrs. Danvers [B] Hedda Gabler [C] Miss Jessel
   [D] Jane Eyre [E] Daisy Miller

10. Anna Karenina leaves her husband for
    [A] Levin [B] Vronsky [C] Oblomov [D] Dmitri
    [E] Bezukhov

22. Wars and Weapons

1. *A Farewell to Arms* by Ernest Hemingway is a novel of
   [A] World War II [B] World War I [C] the Civil War
   [D] the Korean War [E] the Crimean War

2. Ben-Hur's enemy was
   [A] Simonides [B] Messala [C] Marcus [D] Caligula
   [E] Brutus

3. Liam O'Flaherty's novel *The Informer* is concerned with
   [A] World War II [B] the Spanish Civil War
   [C] the Irish Civil War [D] the War of the Roses
   [E] World War I

4. The title of G. B. Shaw's play *Arms and the Man* comes from
   [A] The Bible [B] the *Republic* [C] the *Aeneid*
   [D] the *Odyssey* [E] *The Divine Comedy*

5. The sword Excalibur is associated with
   [A] Alexander the Great [B] Galahad [C] Roland
   [D] Ivanhoe [E] Arthur

6. *The Longest Day* by Cornelius Ryan is an account of
   [A] the Armada [B] 1066 [C] D-Day
   [D] battle of Actium [E] battle of Bull Run

7. A description of the Battle of Waterloo is found in the French novel
   [A] *The Red and the Black*
   [B] *The Charterhouse of Parma* [C] *Madame Bovary*
   [D] *The Counterfeiters* [E] *The Plague*

8. The background of the *Charge of the Light Brigade* by Alfred Lord Tennyson is the
   [A] Korean War [B] War of 1812 [C] Crimean War
   [D] Spanish-American War [E] Civil War

9. Which of these novels is concerned with the atomic bomb?
   [A] *The Armada* [B] *On the Beach* [C] *1984*
   [D] *What Price Glory* [E] *All Quiet on the Western Front*

10. John Steinbeck's book about World War II is
    [A] *The Grapes of Wrath* [B] *Of Mice and Men*
    [C] *East of Eden* [D] *The Moon Is Down*
    [E] *Tortilla Flat*

23. Kinship

1. The son of Cedric the Saxon was
   [A] Lancelot [B] Ivanhoe [C] Arthur [D] Athelstane
   [E] Robin Hood

2. Two writers related to each other are
   [A] Arthur Miller and Henry Miller
   [B] T. E. Lawrence and D. H. Lawrence
   [C] George Eliot and T. S. Eliot
   [D] Osbert Sitwell and Edith Sitwell
   [E] Edward Fitzgerald and F. Scott Fitzgerald

3. The daughters of Père Goriot were
   [A] Camille and Emma   [B] Eugénie and Nanon
   [C] Anastasie and Delphine   [D] Fantine and Cosette
   [E] Alissa and Juliette

4. The uncle of Tristan was
   [A] King Midas   [B] Laius   [C] King Mark
   [D] Charlemagne   [E] Wotan

5. The son of Theseus was
   [A] Hector   [B] Hercules   [C] Perseus   [D] Hippolytus
   [E] Ajax

6. The son of Banquo in *Macbeth* is
   [A] Fleance   [B] Malcolm   [C] Donalbain   [D] Duncan
   [E] Cawdor

7. The daughter of Gervaise was
   [A] Emma   [B] Nana   [C] Camille   [D] Eugénie
   [E] Cosette

8. In *King Lear*, the sister of Regan and Goneril is
   [A] Celia   [B] Cymbeline   [C] Calpurnia   [D] Cordelia
   [E] Olivia

9. The son of Daedalus was
   [A] Perseus   [B] Theseus   [C] Icarus   [D] Hercules
   [E] Orpheus

10. The son of Uther was
    [A] Galahad   [B] Gareth   [C] Lancelot   [D] Arthur
    [E] Gawain

24. Literary Terms

1. *The Rape of the Lock* by Alexander Pope is
   [A] a novel   [B] a play   [C] a mock-epic   [D] a pastoral
   [E] a Gothic tale

2. An unfinished satirical novel about Hollywood is
   [A] *The Great Gatsby*   [B] *The Titan*
   [C] *The Last Tycoon*   [D] *The Last Hurrah*
   [E] *Brave New World*

3. Eudora Welty's book in the form of an extended monologue
   is
   [A] *Delta Wedding*   [B] *The Ponder Heart*
   [C] *The Bride of Innisfallen*   [D] *The Robber Bridegroom*
   [E] *Golden Apples*

4. *The Loved One* by Evelyn Waugh is a satiric novel about
   [A] Hollywood and Forest Lawn
   [B] the London Mayfair set
   [C] the French existentialists   [D] Utopian communities
   [E] the Gothic novel

5. The technical devices the "Newsreel" and the "Camera Eye"
   are associated with the American writer
   [A] John Steinbeck   [B] John Dos Passos   [C] John O'Hara
   [D] John Updike   [E] Truman Capote

6. Robert Browning's *The Ring and the Book* is an example of
   [A] allegory   [B] morality play
   [C] series of dramatic monologues   [D] epic   [E] lyric poem

7. John Milton's *Comus* is a
   [A] sonnet   [B] pastoral   [C] masque   [D] rondeau
   [E] saga

8. One of the characteristics of the Romantics was an interest in
   [A] Roman culture   [B] industrialism   [C] communism
   [D] medieval culture   [E] haiku

9. Sir Philip Sidney's *Arcadia* is an example of the
   [A] sonnet   [B] allegory   [C] pastoral   [D] ode   [E] epic

10. An Icelandic prose narrative is called
    [A] a satire   [B] a sonnet   [C] a saga   [D] an idyll
    [E] a sotie

25. Religion and Philosophy

1. The essay *Self-Reliance* is by
   [A] Henry David Thoreau   [B] R. L. Stevenson
   [C] Francis Bacon   [D] Ralph Waldo Emerson
   [E] Aldous Huxley

2. The terms "will to power" and "superman" are associated
   with
   [A] Kant   [B] Hegel   [C] Schopenhauer   [D] Nietzsche
   [E] Schleiermacher

3. The philosopher who wrote *The Last Puritan* is
   [A] William James   [B] Henri Bergson   [C] Benedetto Croce
   [D] Bertrand Russell   [E] George Santayana

4. *Sturm und Drang* in Germany was a movement of
   [A] pessimism   [B] religious revival   [C] youthful revolt
   [D] neo-classicism   [E] didactic poetry

5. In his *Moral Discourses*, Epictetus sets forth the doctrine of
   [A] Hedonism   [B] Epicureanism   [C] Stoicism
   [D] Paganism   [E] Idealism

6. The minister in *The Scarlet Letter* by Nathaniel Hawthorne
   is
   [A] Roger Chillingworth   [B] Arthur Dimmesdale
   [C] Clifford Pyncheon   [D] Goodman Brown
   [E] Ethan Frome

7. The philosopher who said, "I think, therefore I am," is
[A] Henri Bergson   [B] George Berkeley
[C] Immanuel Kant   [D] Henry James
[E] René Descartes

8. The High Lama appears in the novel
[A] *A Passage to India*   [B] *The Light That Failed*
[C] *Siddhartha*   [D] *Lost Horizon*   [E] *The Rains Came*

9. Thomas à Kempis wrote
[A] *Utopia*   [B] *City of God*   [C] *The Little Flowers*
[D] *The Imitation of Christ*   [E] *Pensées*

10. Monseigneur Myriel is a bishop in
[A] *The Keys of the Kingdom*   [B] *Barchester Towers*
[C] *Les Misérables*   [D] *The Devil's Advocate*
[E] *The Cardinal*

26. Where Are We?

1. Sweet Auburn is the name of the village in
[A] *Rasselas*   [B] *Jude the Obscure*
[C] *The Vicar of Wakefield*   [D] *The Deserted Village*
[E] *Spoon River Anthology*

2. The action of *The Comedy of Errors* take place in
[A] Rhodes   [B] Ephesus   [C] Knossos   [D] Athens
[E] Sparta

3. Passepartout accompanies Phileas Fogg
[A] to the theatre   [B] to the races   [C] on a yacht cruise
[D] around the world   [E] on a safari

4. The Joads in *The Grapes of Wrath* by John Steinbeck migrate
from the dust-bowl area to
[A] Mexico   [B] Chicago   [C] New Orleans   [D] Texas
[E] California

5. The school from which Holden Caulfield flees is
   [A] Chauncey   [B] Pencey   [C] Brookfield
   [D] Stoughton   [E] Merton

6. Nicholas Nickleby secures a position at
   [A] Brookfield   [B] Pencey   [C] Tintern Abbey
   [D] Dotheboys Hall   [E] Haddon Hall

7. The action of *The Bridge of San Luis Rey* by Thornton Wilder
   takes place in
   [A] Mexico   [B] Bolivia   [C] Spain   [D] Peru
   [E] Argentina

8. The *Ramayana* is part of the epic literature of
   [A] Russia   [B] Portugal   [C] Norway   [D] Greece
   [E] India

9. The setting of *The Marble Faun* by Nathaniel Hawthorne is
   [A] Salem   [B] Boston   [C] Paris   [D] Italy   [E] Spain

10. Lochinvar came out of the West to
    [A] Haddon Hall   [B] Thornfield   [C] Manderley
    [D] Netherby Hall   [E] Tara

27. Novels

1. A novel by Muriel Spark whose theme is "gerontology" is
   [A] *A Severed Head*   [B] *A Burnt-out Case*
   [C] *Memento Mori*   [D] *Room at the Top*   [E] *Lucky Jim*

2. Dick Heldar is an artist in
   [A] *Lust for Life*   [B] *The Moon and Sixpence*
   [C] *Of Human Bondage*   [D] *The Light That Failed*
   [E] *Doctor Faustus*

3. An early novel of Vladimir Nabokov is
   [A] *Oblomov*   [B] *Dead Souls*   [C] *The Gift*
   [D] *The Possessed*   [E] *Fathers and Sons*

4. Budd Schulberg wrote
   [A] *The Tunnel of Love*   [B] *The Groves of Academe*
   [C] *What Makes Sammy Run?*
   [D] *A Death in the Family*   [E] *The Day of the Locust*

5. Jack Kerouac's well-known novel is
   [A] *A Rage to Live*   [B] *On the Road*
   [C] *Breakfast at Tiffany's*   [D] *Clock without Hands*
   [E] *Fanny Hill*

6. Katherine Anne Porter wrote
   [A] *The Group*   [B] *To Kill a Mocking-bird*
   [C] *Elizabeth Appleton*   [D] *Ship of Fools*
   [E] *The Child Buyers*

7. One of the Cowperwood novels by Theodore Dreiser is
   [A] *Manhattan Transfer*   [B] *Appointment in Samarra*
   [C] *The Titan*   [D] *The Sound and the Fury*
   [E] *The Web and the Rock*

8. A novel whose locale is "Wessex" is
   [A] *Middlemarch*   [B] *The Sound and the Fury*
   [C] *The Return of the Native*   [D] *1984*
   [E] *Ivanhoe*

9. Carson McCullers' novel which begins: "An army post in
   peace-time is a dull place" is
   [A] *The Ballad of the Sad Café*
   [B] *The Member of the Wedding*
   [C] *The Heart Is a Lonely Hunter*
   [D] *Reflections in a Golden Eye*   [E] *Clock without Hands*

10. The phrase "President of the Immortals" appears at the end
    of
    [A] *Esther Waters*   [B] *Cousin Bette*
    [C] *Tess of the D'Urbervilles*   [D] *Moby Dick*
    [E] *Don Quixote*

28. Guess the Author

1. The author of *The List of Adrian Messenger* is
   [A] Hugh Pentecost   [B] Michael Innes
   [C] Patrick Quentin   [D] Philip MacDonald
   [E] Marjorie Allingham

2. The novel about a nymphet is by
   [A] John Steinbeck   [B] Booth Tarkington
   [C] John O'Hara   [D] Vladimir Nabokov
   [E] Thornton Wilder

3. John Rechy is the author of
   [A] *Tender Is the Night*   [B] *City of Night*
   [C] *Fanny Hill*   [D] *Lie Down in Darkness*
   [E] *Another Country*

4. The author of *Raise High the Roof Beam, Carpenters* is
   [A] John Updike   [B] Truman Capote   [C] Mary McCarthy
   [D] William Styron   [E] J. D. Salinger

5. A writer who has written both novels and biographies is
   [A] Catherine Drinker Bowen   [B] James Boswell
   [C] André Maurois   [D] Van Wyck Brooks
   [E] Emil Ludwig

6. John Steinbeck is the author of
   [A] *Travels with Charley*   [B] *Aspects of the Novel*
   [C] *Common Sense*   [D] *Hiroshima*   [E] *Exile's Return*

7. The author of *On the Beach* is
   [A] William Golding   [B] C. P. Snow   [C] Nevil Shute
   [D] Richard Hughes   [E] Kingsley Amis

8. "Markheim" is a short story by
   [A] Henry James   [B] Edgar Allan Poe
   [C] Robert Louis Stevenson   [D] Joseph Conrad
   [E] Aldous Huxley

9. The author of books about John Milton and T. E. Lawrence
is
[A] J. D. Salinger   [B] John O'Hara   [C] Aldous Huxley
[D] Robert Graves   [E] Hermann Hesse

10. The author of *The Fox in the Attic* is
[A] Auberon Waugh   [B] John Braine   [C] Richard Hughes
[D] Graham Greene   [E] John Wain

29. The Theatre

1. Vladimir and Estragon appear in Samuel Beckett's play
[A] *Endgame*   [B] *Krapp's Last Tape*   [C] *All that Fall*
[D] *Waiting for Godot*   [E] *Molloy*

2. The "Italian Molière" was
[A] Alfieri   [B] Boccaccio   [C] Goldoni   [D] Pirandello
[E] Manzoni

3. Regina Giddens is the central character of Lillian Hellman's
play
[A] *The Children's Hour*   [B] *The Autumn Garden*
[C] *The Watch on the Rhine*   [D] *The Little Foxes*
[C] *Candide*

4. A silver bullet plays a role in Eugene O'Neill's play
[A] *Anna Christie*   [B] *The Hairy Ape*
[C] *Emperor Jones*   [D] *Strange Interlude*
[E] *Mourning Becomes Electra*

5. Mosca and Corbaccio are characters in
[A] *The Alchemist*   [B] *She Stoops to Conquer*
[C] *Volpone*   [D] *The Rivals*   [E] *The Comedy of Errors*

6. The date 31,920 A.D. is found in G. B. Shaw's play
[A] *Saint Joan*   [B] *Heartbreak House*
[C] *Man and Superman*   [D] *Back to Methuselah*
[E] *Caesar and Cleopatra*

7. Friedrich Schiller wrote
   [A] *Faust* [B] *Dr. Faustus* [C] *Nathan the Wise*
   [D] *William Tell* [E] *In Praise of Folly*

8. Lorraine Hansberry is the author of the play
   [A] *Porgy and Bess* [B] *Green Pastures*
   [C] *A Raisin in the Sun* [D] *Purlie Victorious*
   [E] *Black Nativity*

9. A modern play about Thomas à Becket is
   [A] *A Man for All Seasons* [B] *J. B.* [C] *Luther*
   [D] *Ross* [E] *Murder in the Cathedral*

10. Willy Loman is a character in the play
    [A] *Sweet Bird of Youth* [B] *Bus Stop* [C] *J. B.*
    [D] *Toys in the Attic* [E] *Death of a Salesman*

30. Main Characters

1. The leading character in *Another Country* by James Baldwin
   is
   [A] Bigger Thomas [B] Emperor Jones [C] Joe Christmas
   [D] James Wait [E] Rufus Scott

2. The hero of *Sons and Lovers* by D. H. Lawrence is
   [A] Dick Diver [B] Paul Morel [C] Andrew Manson
   [D] Clyde Griffiths [E] Gulley Jimson

3. Nicholas Rubashov is the central character of
   [A] *The Trial* [B] *The Idiot* [C] *Darkness at Noon*
   [D] *The Age of Reason* [E] *Freedom or Death*

4. Axel Heyst is the hero of
   [A] *Victory* [B] *The Trial* [C] *Darkness at Noon*
   [D] *Man's Hope* [E] *Room at the Top*

5. Diggory Venn appears in
   [A] *Wuthering Heights*   [B] *The Mill on the Floss*
   [C] *The Return of the Native*   [D] *Bleak House*
   [E] *Mansfield Park*

6. Nessim and Narouz Hosnani appear in the novel
   [A] *A Passage to India*   [B] *Mountolive*   [C] *Hawaii*
   [D] *Caravans*   [E] *Cry, the Beloved Country*

7. The narrator in the novels of C. P. Snow is
   [A] Mark Rampion   [B] Major Scobie
   [C] Gulley Jimson   [D] Lewis Eliot   [E] Joe Lampton

8. Lanny Budd is the hero of
   [A] *Dragon Seed*   [B] *Dragon's Teeth*   [C] *Oliver Wiswell*
   [D] *Barren Ground*   [E] *World Enough and Time*

9. Ian Fleming is the creator of
   [A] Philip Marlowe   [B] Philo Vance
   [C] Inspector Alleyn   [D] James Bond
   [E] Inspector Maigret

10. In *The Prince and the Pauper* by Mark Twain, the Pauper's
    name was
    [A] Tom Jones   [B] Pons   [C] Holden Caulfield
    [D] Sam   [E] Tom Canty

31. Supporting Figures

1. Don Quixote chose as his lady a peasant girl named
   [A] Esmeralda   [B] Carmen   [C] Isabella   [D] Dulcinea
   [E] Doña Perfecta

2. Mrs. Grose is the housekeeper in
   [A] *Rebecca*   [B] *David Copperfield*
   [C] *Wuthering Heights*   [D] *The Turn of the Screw*
   [E] *Vanity Fair*

3. The man-about-town in James Joyce's *Ulysses* is
   [A] Stephen Dedalus   [B] Buck Mulligan
   [C] Leopold Bloom   [D] Blazes Boylan
   [E] Humphrey Earwicker

4. Elizabeth Bennet appears in
   [A] *Vanity Fair*   [B] *Pride and Prejudice*
   [C] *The Old Wives' Tale*   [D] *Jane Eyre*
   [E] *The Mayor of Casterbridge*

5. Dr. Gottlieb is a character in
   [A] *The Citadel*   [B] *Not as a Stranger*   [C] *Arrowsmith*
   [D] *The Plague*   [E] *The Magic Mountain*

6. In *The Song of Roland*, the hero's comrade is
   [A] Raoul   [B] Turpin   [C] Charlemagne   [D] Olivier
   [E] Ganelon

7. Blaise Meredith appears in the novel
   [A] *The Unicorn*   [B] *The Centaur*   [C] *The Group*
   [D] *The Devil's Advocate*   [E] *Elizabeth Appleton*

8. The gypsy girl in *The Hunchback of Notre Dame* by Victor
   Hugo is called
   [A] Carmen   [B] Lolita   [C] Virginia   [D] Esmeralda
   [E] Dulcinea

9. Schoolmaster Squeers appears in the novel
   [A] *The Corn Is Green*   [B] *The Masters*
   [C] *Good-bye, Mr. Chips*   [D] *Nicholas Nickleby*
   [E] *The Browning Version*

10. Professor Bhaer appears in
    [A] *The Masters*   [B] *The Corn Is Green*
    [C] *Little Women*   [D] *The Groves of Academe*   [E] *Pnin*

32. It's All Relative

1. In the book *Ethan Frome* by Edith Wharton, Mattie and
   Zeena are
   [A] sisters   [B] mother and daughter   [C] cousins
   [D] mistress and servant   [E] wife and sister-in-law

2. The name of the family in *Tobacco Road* by Erskine Caldwell
   is
   [A] Snopes   [B] Sloper   [C] Lester   [D] Joad
   [E] Caulfield

3. Ernest, Francis, Fritz and Jack belong to
   [A] the Pontifex family   [B] the Joad family
   [C] the Robinson family   [D] the Compson family
   [E] the Gant family

4. The mother of Pearl was
   [A] Moll Flanders   [B] Sadie Thompson
   [C] Hester Prynne   [D] Mrs. Bennet   [E] Mattie Silver

5. In *A Midsummer Night's Dream*, the daughter of Egeus is
   [A] Helena   [B] Hermia   [C] Thisbe   [D] Viola   [E] Portia

6. The Pontifex family appears in the novel
   [A] *Little Women*   [B] *Buddenbrooks*
   [C] *The Counterfeiters*   [D] *The Way of All Flesh*
   [E] *Vanity Fair*

7. Steve, Daisy, Helen, Ben and Luke are the children of
   [A] Mr. Pontifex   [B] Mr. Bennet   [C] Mr. Gant
   [D] Mr. Joad   [E] Mr. Micawber

8. The brother of Dmitri and Alyosha is
   [A] Pierre   [B] Oblomov   [C] Stavrogin   [D] Ivan
   [E] Fyodor

9. Moses, Olivia, George and Sophia are the children of
   [A] Judge Pyncheon   [B] Mrs. Bennet   [C] Mr. Pontifex
   [D] Squire Western   [E] Dr. Primrose

10. Manuel and Esteban are twins in
    [A] *Don Quixote*   [B] *Tortilla Flat*
    [C] *The Bridge of San Luis Rey*   [D] *Colomba*
    [E] *Carmen*

33. Science Fiction and the Unknown

1. Martians appear in
   [A] *Wuthering Heights*   [B] *The Moonstone*
   [C] *The War of the Worlds*   [D] *The Good Earth*
   [E] *The Four Horsemen of the Apocalypse*

2. *Behemoth* and *Leviathan* are the titles of works by
   [A] Herman Melville   [B] Jacques-Yves Cousteau
   [C] Thomas Merton   [D] Thomas Hobbes   [E] G. F. Hegel

3. A pioneer of science fiction is
   [A] James Fenimore Cooper   [B] Henry James
   [C] H. G. Wells   [D] Washington Irving
   [E] Anthony Trollope

4. The creator of *Dr. Lao* is
   [A] Ian Fleming   [B] H. G. Wells   [C] Sax Rohmer
   [D] Charles Finney   [E] Isaac Asimov

5. Epsilons and Alphas appear in Aldous Huxley's novel
   [A] *Point Counter Point*   [B] *Brave New World*
   [C] *Antic Hay*   [D] *Crome Yellow*   [E] *Eyeless in Gaza*

6. The author of *Tales from the White Hart* is
   [A] Ray Bradbury   [B] Theodore Sturgeon
   [C] Isaac Asimov   [D] H. G. Wells   [E] Arthur C. Clarke

7. The author of *Martian Chronicles* is
   [A] Jules Verne   [B] H. G. Wells   [C] Bram Stoker
   [D] Oscar Wilde   [E] Ray Bradbury

8. The imaginary land of *The Prisoner of Zenda* by Anthony Hope is
   [A] Graustark   [B] Ruritania   [C] Oceania
   [D] Poictesme   [E] Shangri-La

9. Morgan le Fay carried Arthur to
   [A] Camelot   [B] Joyous Guard   [C] Castle Garden
   [D] Avalon   [E] the Castle of Otranto

10. Winston Smith is the hero of the novel
    [A] *Brave New World*   [B] *Burmese Days*   [C] *1984*
    [D] *The Time Machine*   [E] *Looking Backward*

34. Places

1. Miles and Flora lived with their governess at
   [A] Otranto   [B] Bracebridge Hall   [C] Bly
   [D] Lamb House   [E] Bleak House

2. Tess is found by the police at
   [A] home   [B] Talbothays   [C] Stonehenge   [D] Sandbourne
   [E] Egdon Heath

3. The excursion to the Marabar Caves takes place in
   [A] *The Dark Labyrinth*   [B] *Tom Sawyer*
   [C] *A Passage to India*   [D] the *Odyssey*   [E] *The Trial*

4. George Eliot's novel set in Renaissance Florence is
   [A] *Middlemarch*   [B] *Daniel Deronda*   [C] *Ramona*
   [D] *Romola*   [E] *Adam Bede*

5. The title character in *McTeague* by Frank Norris dies in
   [A] the Black Forest   [B] the Catskills
   [C] a railway station   [D] Death Valley   [E] the Dead Sea

6. The action of *Mister Roberts* by Thomas Heggen takes place
[A] on an island   [B] on a yacht   [C] in a camp
[D] on a cargo ship   [E] in a naval academy

7. *Borstal Boy* is Brendan Behan's account of his three years
[A] in the army   [B] in a private school
[C] in a government office   [D] in a reformatory
[E] in the theatre

8. The Bennet girls lived at
[A] Netherby Hall   [B] Thornfield
[C] Netherfield Park   [D] Tara   [E] Manderley

9. *The Day of the Locust* by Nathanael West is a novel about
[A] Broadway   [B] China   [C] Paris
[D] Greenwich Village   [E] Hollywood

10. The place from which Chaucer's characters set out was
[A] Mermaid Tavern   [B] Tabard Inn   [C] Globe Theatre
[D] Trafalgar Square   [E] Victoria Station

35. Literary Style

1. The "Vinteuil Sonata" is used as a leitmotif in
[A] *The Immoralist*   [B] *The Plague*   [C] *Nausea*
[D] *The Mandarins*   [E] *Remembrance of Things Past*

2. The title *Chu Chin Chow* is an example of
[A] metonomy   [B] polysyndeton   [C] alliteration
[D] chiasmus   [E] hysteron proteron

3. The term that describes *The Castle of Otranto* by Horace
Walpole is
[A] romantic   [B] realistic   [C] gothic   [D] symbolistic
[E] allegorical

4. An example of an epistolary novel is
[A] *The Loved One*   [B] *The Bull from the Sea*
[C] *The Ides of March*   [D] *The Masters*   [E] *Ethan Frome*

5. The *Iliad* is written in
[A] alexandrines [B] rhymed couplets
[C] dactylic hexameter [D] trochaic trimeter
[E] adonic verse

6. Graham Greene calls some of his novels
[A] "mysteries" [B] "horror stories"
[C] "entertainments" [D] "spy thrillers"
[E] "science fiction"

7. *Against the Grain*, by J. K. Huysmans, is an example of the
style of the
[A] classicists [B] romantics [C] decadents
[D] expressionists [E] surrealists

8. Thomas Hardy's expression for chance or coincidence is
[A] Kismet [B] Fate [C] Hap [D] Moira [E] Hubris

9. *The Sorrows of Young Werther* by Goethe is
[A] a picaresque novel [B] an epistolary novel
[C] a gothic novel [D] a Zolaesque novel [E] an allegory

10. The *Kalevala* is
[A] a Spanish drama [B] an Italian lyric poem
[C] a Finnish epic [D] a Hindu poem [E] an Arabian tale

36. Disasters

1. "I was killed i' the Capitol; Brutus killed me," is a line from
[A] *Antony and Cleopatra* [B] *Caesar and Cleopatra*
[C] *Julius Caesar* [D] *Hamlet* [E] *Macbeth*

2. The Giant Despair appears in
[A] the *Odyssey* [B] *Everyman* [C] *Beowulf*
[D] *The Pilgrim's Progress* [E] *Idylls of the King*

3. *Death in the Afternoon* by Ernest Hemingway is about
[A] a plague [B] a battle [C] an execution
[D] an explosion [E] bullfighting

4. Jessica Mitford wrote
   [A] *The Loved One*   [B] *Death and Transfiguration*
   [C] *Man Against Death*   [D] *The American Way of Death*
   [E] *Death in Venice*

5. The Four Horsemen of the Apocalypse are death, war,
   pestilence and
   [A] fire   [B] flood   [C] famine   [D] torture   [E] slavery

6. The author of *The Day Lincoln was Shot* is
   [A] Bernard De Voto   [B] Mark Van Doren
   [C] Louis Hacker   [D] James A. Bishop
   [E] Henry Commager

7. The fire at Manderley was set by
   [A] Max de Winter   [B] Rebecca
   [C] the second Mrs. de Winter   [D] Mrs. Danvers
   [E] a pyromaniac

8. The heel of Achilles was
   [A] broken   [B] immune   [C] sprained   [D] vulnerable
   [E] bound

9. Agamemnon sacrificed his daughter
   [A] Electra   [B] Cassandra   [C] Iphigenia
   [D] Antigone   [E] Ariadne

10. *Death in Venice* by Thomas Mann is set against a background
    of
    [A] an accident   [B] an explosion   [C] a poisoning
    [D] a plague   [E] a shooting

37. Miscellaneous Writers

1. "The Champion" is a short story by
   [A] Damon Runyon   [B] Ring Lardner
   [C] Truman Capote   [D] Shirley Jackson   [E] Saki

2. The author of *Elizabeth Appleton* is
   [A] John O'Hara   [B] Rumer Godden
   [C] Helen MacInnes   [D] John Updike   [E] Norman Mailer

3. Albert Camus is the author of
   [A] *The Myth of Sisyphus*   [B] *No Exit*
   [C] *The Counterfeiters*   [D] *Man's Fate*   [E] *The Rehearsal*

4. "The Cop and the Anthem" is a well-known short story by
   [A] Sherwood Anderson   [B] O. Henry   [C] Truman Capote
   [D] Shirley Jackson   [E] James Joyce

5. The author of *And Quiet Flows the Don* is
   [A] Tolstoy   [B] Dostoevsky   [C] Gorki   [D] Sholokhov
   [E] Chekhov

6. *Oliver Wiswell* is a historical novel by
   [A] Thomas Costain   [B] Kenneth Roberts
   [C] Charles Dickens   [D] George Orwell   [E] Alan Paton

7. The author of *The Maltese Falcon* is
   [A] Raymond Chandler   [B] Rex Stout
   [C] Erle Stanley Gardner   [D] Dashiell Hammett
   [E] Hugh Pentecost

8. The author of *The Little Prince* is
   [A] Mark Twain   [B] Terence Rattigan   [C] Saint-Exupéry
   [D] Lewis Carroll   [E] Felix Salten

9. An author who was formerly a philosophy don at Oxford is
   [A] Rumer Godden   [B] Muriel Spark   [C] Iris Murdoch
   [D] Elizabeth Bowen   [E] Shelagh Delaney

10. Bram Stoker is the author of
    [A] *The Werewolf of London*   [B] *Frankenstein*   [C] *Dracula*
    [D] *The Lady in White*   [E] "The Willows"

38. Myths and Legends

1. The Naiads were
   [A] mountain nymphs   [B] forest nymphs
   [C] water nymphs   [D] fates   [E] Graces

2. The winged horse of mythology was
   [A] the Centaur   [B] Bellerophon   [C] Pegasus
   [D] the Hydra   [E] the Gorgon

3. The Norse goddess of Love and Beauty was
   [A] Frigga   [B] Valhalla   [C] Freya   [D] Urda   [E] Edda

4. The house of Atreus was cursed by
   [A] Clytemnestra   [B] Thyestes   [C] Agamemnon
   [D] Orestes   [E] Cassandra

5. The Queen of the Lower World was
   [A] Hera   [B] Artemis   [C] Hestia   [D] Persephone
   [E] Eurydice

6. The giants with one great eye were
   [A] the Titans   [B] the Cyclopes   [C] the Furies
   [D] the Fates   [E] the Harpies

7. The god Neptune always carried his
   [A] sword   [B] wand   [C] baton   [D] cane   [E] trident

8. The man who forever tries to roll a stone uphill is
   [A] Tantalus   [B] Sisyphus   [C] Prometheus
   [D] Eteocles   [E] Teiresias

9. The King of the Winds was
   [A] Eurus   [B] Boreas   [C] Aeolus   [D] Notus   [E] Zephyr

10. The boatman of the lower world was called
    [A] Cerberus   [B] Minos   [C] Pluto   [D] Charon
    [E] Phlegethon

39. Drama

1. Edward Albee made a stage adaptation of Carson McCullers'
   book
   [A] *Clock without Hands*   [B] *The Member of the Wedding*
   [c] *Reflections in a Golden Eye*
   [D] *The Ballad of the Sad Café*
   [E] *The Heart is a Lonely Hunter*

2. Big Daddy appears in the play
   [A] *A View from the Bridge*   [B] *The Ballad of the Sad Café*
   [c] *Cat on a Hot Tin Roof*   [D] *A Raisin in the Sun*
   [E] *All My Sons*

3. Dr. Stockmann is a character in Henrik Ibsen's play
   [A] *Brand*   [B] *Hedda Gabler*   [c] *A Doll's House*
   [D] *Rosmersholm*   [E] *An Enemy of the People*

4. The pen name of Jean-Baptiste Poquelin is
   [A] Voltaire   [B] Honoré de Balzac   [c] Albert Camus
   [D] Molière   [E] François Rabelais

5. The author of *The Caretaker* is
   [A] Jean Genet   [B] Edward Albee   [c] Eugène Ionesco
   [D] Harold Pinter   [E] Bertolt Brecht

6. Nora Helmer is a character in
   [A] *The Little Foxes*   [B] *Hedda Gabler*   [c] *The Rivals*
   [D] *A Doll's House*   [E] *The Glass Menagerie*

7. The dramatist whose theatre illustrates the contrast between
   illusion and reality is
   [A] Richard Sheridan   [B] Jean Racine
   [c] G. B. Shaw   [D] Luigi Pirandello   [E] Sean O'Casey

8. Christopher Fry's play about Henry II and Becket is
   [A] *Venus Observed*   [B] *A Sleep of Prisoners*
   [c] *The Dark is Light Enough*   [D] *Curtmantle*
   [E] *The Lady's Not for Burning*

9. G. B. Shaw derived his belief of the Life Force from the philosopher
[A] Plato   [B] G. F. Hegel   [C] Immanuel Kant
[D] Henri Bergson   [E] Arthur Schopenhauer

10. Hesione Hushabye is a character in G. B. Shaw's play
[A] *Candida*   [B] *Pygmalion*   [C] *Man and Superman*
[D] *Heartbreak House*   [E] *Major Barbara*

40. Poets

1. The author of the *Rowley Poems* was
[A] Thomas Gray   [B] Oliver Goldsmith
[C] James Thomson   [D] Thomas Chatterton
[E] Samuel Johnson

2. The elegy about John Keats is
[A] "Thyrsis"   [B] "Adonais"   [C] "Lycidas"
[D] "Endymion"   [E] "Enoch Arden"

3. The poet who wrote *The Necessity of Atheism* is
[A] Byron   [B] Shelley   [C] Keats   [D] Tennyson
[E] Whitman

4. Henry Wadsworth Longfellow wrote
[A] "Lilacs"   [B] *Evangeline*   [C] *Leaves of Grass*
[D] "Thanatopsis"   [E] "Concord Hymn"

5. One of the Metaphysical poets is
[A] John Keats   [B] Stephen Spender   [C] John Milton
[D] Algernon Swinburne   [E] John Donne

6. Robert Lowell wrote
[A] *The Waste Land*   [B] *The Age of Anxiety*
[C] *John Brown's Body*   [D] *Lord Weary's Castle*
[E] *Holes in the Sky*

7. Dante Gabriel Rossetti was a poet of the
   [A] Gothic school   [B] Symbolist school
   [C] Romantic school   [D] Pre-Raphaelite school
   [E] Realistic school

8. T. S. Eliot wrote
   [A] "Memorial Rain"   [B] "Lilacs"
   [C] "The Hollow Men"   [D] "Invictus"   [E] "The Soldier"

9. The terms "inscape" and "instress" are associated with the poet
   [A] T. S. Eliot   [B] Alfred Lord Tennyson   [C] John Keats
   [D] W. H. Auden   [E] Gerard Manley Hopkins

10. *Les Illuminations* is the work of French poet
    [A] Verlaine   [B] Baudelaire   [C] Rimbaud   [D] Claudel
    [E] Mallarmé

41. Who Wrote ...?

1. Herman Wouk wrote
   [A] *Caravans*   [B] *Youngblood Hawke*
   [C] *Kingsblood Royal*   [D] *Gideon Planish*
   [E] *Martin Eden*

2. Maurice Herzog's well-known book is
   [A] *Kon-tiki*   [B] *The Dead Sea Scrolls*   [C] *Annapurna*
   [D] *The Armada*   [E] *Cybernetics*

3. T. E. Lawrence wrote
   [A] *Travels in Arabia Deserta*   [B] *The Garden of Allah*
   [C] *The Sheltering Sky*   [D] *Revolt in the Desert*
   [E] *East of Eden*

4. Iris Murdoch's gothic novel is
   [A] *The Bell*   [B] *A Severed Head*   [C] *The Unicorn*
   [D] *The Sandcastle*   [E] *Under the Net*

5. Pierre Boulle wrote
   [A] *The Quiet Man*   [B] *Man's Hope*
   [C] *A View from the Bridge*
   [D] *The Bridge over the River Kwai*   [E] *Ship of Fools*

6. John Dos Passos wrote
   [A] *1984*   [B] *7½ cents*   [C] *1066 and All That*   [D] *1919*
   [E] *Ninety-three*

7. John Marquand wrote
   [A] *The Big Money*   [B] *Wickford Point*
   [C] *Between Two Worlds*   [D] *Martin Eden*   [E] *The Pit*

8. Philip Quarles' notebook appears in the Aldous Huxley novel
   [A] *Crome Yellow*   [B] *Antic Hay*   [C] *Eyeless in Gaza*
   [D] *Point Counter Point*   [E] *Brave New World*

9. Vincent Sheean wrote
   [A] *Franny and Zooey*   [B] *My Darling Clementine*
   [C] *Dorothy and Red*   [D] *Lord Jim*
   [E] *My Cousin Rachel*

10. James Gould Cozzens wrote
    [A] *The Winter of Our Discontent*   [B] *The Glass Blowers*
    [C] *The Centaur*   [D] *By Love Possessed*
    [E] *Delta Wedding*

42. Leading Figures

1. The fictional character who lived at 221B Baker Street is
   [A] Dr. Jekyll   [B] Hester Prynne
   [C] Sherlock Holmes   [D] Becky Sharp
   [E] Lord Peter Wimsey

2. The hero of *Look Homeward, Angel* by Thomas Wolfe is
   [A] Dick Diver   [B] Joe Christmas   [C] Eugene Gant
   [D] Tom Joad   [E] George Webber

3. John Dickson Carr is the creator of the detective
   [A] Hercule Poirot [B] Nero Wolfe [C] Dupin
   [D] Dr. Gideon Fell [E] Jane Marple

4. The hero of Upton Sinclair's series of novels is
   [A] Studs Lonigan [B] Henry Fleming [C] Frederick Henry
   [D] Dick Diver [E] Lanny Budd

5. The boy who is "kidnapped" in R. L. Stevenson's novel is
   [A] Jim Hawkins [B] Holden Caulfield
   [C] Joe the fat boy [D] David Balfour [E] Miles

6. Amory Blaine is the hero of
   [A] *Tender Is the Night* [B] *The Last Tycoon*
   [C] *The Great Gatsby* [D] *The Beautiful and Damned*
   [E] *This Side of Paradise*

7. Philip Carey is the hero of
   [A] *Green Mansions* [B] *Kim* [C] *The Innocent Voyage*
   [D] *Lord of the Flies* [E] *Of Human Bondage*

8. The protagonist of *All the King's Men* by Robert Penn Warren
   is
   [A] Willy Loman [B] George Hurstwood
   [C] Willie Stark [D] Quentin Compson
   [E] Gideon Planish

9. The hero of *Lorna Doone* by Richard D. Blackmore is
   [A] Angel Clare [B] Rawdon Crawley [C] Charles II
   [D] John Ridd [E] Colonel Jack

10. The pupil of Dr. Pangloss is
    [A] D'Artagnan [B] Candide [C] Javert [D] Topaze
    [E] Lafcadio

43. Settings

1. The setting of *A Bell for Adano* by John Hersey is
   [A] Peru [B] Spain [C] Italy [D] Brazil [E] Mexico

2. The action of *Native Son* by Richard Wright takes place in
   [A] New Orleans   [B] Boston   [C] Chicago
   [D] New York   [E] San Francisco

3. The setting of Gustave Flaubert's *Salammbo* is
   [A] Rome   [B] Athens   [C] Carthage
   [D] Alexandria   [E] Mecca

4. *From Here to Eternity* by James Jones is a novel of Army life in
   [A] Germany   [B] Korea   [C] the Philippines
   [D] Hawaii   [E] a camp in the United States

5. The setting of Albert Camus' novel *The Fall* is
   [A] Oran   [B] Algiers   [C] Paris   [D] Amsterdam
   [E] Rome

6. Pitcairn's Island appears in
   [A] *Treasure Island*   [B] *Moby Dick*   [C] *The Sea Wolf*
   [D] *Mutiny on the Bounty*   [E] *The Caine Mutiny*

7. The setting of *Justine* and *Balthazar* by Lawrence Durrell is
   [A] Paris   [B] Rome   [C] Alexandria   [D] Athens
   [E] London

8. The scene of *Another Country* by James Baldwin is
   [A] New Orleans   [B] Germany   [C] Chicago
   [D] New York   [E] Hollywood

9. The setting of Malraux's *Man's Fate* is
   [A] Spain   [B] France   [C] Italy   [D] China
   [E] Germany

10. The action of *The Magic Mountain* by Thomas Mann takes place in
    [A] a hotel   [B] a private school   [C] a sanatorium
    [D] a private home   [E] a castle

44. Professions

1. Doctor Faustus in Thomas Mann's novel of the same name is a
   [A] physicist [B] professor [C] lawyer [D] composer
   [E] philosopher

2. In *The Scarlet Letter*, by Nathaniel Hawthorne, Roger Chillingworth was
   [A] a physician [B] a minister [C] a scholar
   [D] a banker [E] a lawyer

3. Svengali's pupil Trilby became
   [A] a dancer [B] a pianist [C] a singer [D] a novelist
   [E] a blacksmith

4. The squire of Don Quixote was
   [A] Pancho Villa [B] El Greco [C] Sancho Panza
   [D] Lazarillo de Tormes [E] Amadis de Gaula

5. Bergotte the author and Berma the actress appear in
   [A] *The Fall* [B] *Jean-Christophe*
   [C] *Remembrance of Things Past* [D] *The Counterfeiters*
   [E] *Chéri*

6. Sherlock Holmes' landlady is
   [A] Mrs. Alving [B] Mrs. Bennet [C] Mrs. Grose
   [D] Mrs. Hudson [E] Mrs. Danvers

7. The American reporter in *The Sun Also Rises* by Ernest Hemingway is
   [A] Michael Campbell [B] Robert Cohn [C] Jake Barnes
   [D] Brett Ashley [E] Cyril Fielding

8. In Alberto Moravia's novel *The Conformist*, Marcello becomes
   [A] a priest [B] a captain [C] a doctor [D] a fascist spy
   [E] a thief

9. Aesculapius was
[A] a poet   [B] a physician   [C] a musician   [D] a shepherd
[E] a blacksmith

10. Lady Chatterley's Lover is
[A] a chauffeur   [B] an artist   [C] a gamekeeper
[D] an actor   [E] a soldier

45. Shorter Works

1. Lord Chesterfield's famous letters were written to
[A] the king   [B] his mother   [C] the queen   [D] his son
[E] his teacher

2. The manual for the Renaissance gentleman was
[A] *The Prince*   [B] *Utopia*   [C] *The Courtier*
[D] *Piers Plowman*   [E] *The Divine Comedy*

3. The author of the newspaper article *"I Accuse"* ("J'Accuse")
was
[A] Honoré de Balzac   [B] Victor Hugo   [C] Émile Zola
[D] Albert Camus   [E] Jean-Paul Sartre

4. The sonnets of Petrarch were inspired by
[A] Beatrice   [B] Fiammetta   [C] Laura   [D] Cornelia
[E] Julia

5. Shirley Jackson is the author of
[A] *Delta Wedding*   [B] *Clock without Hands*
[C] *The Lottery*   [D] *Dubliners*   [E] *A Tree of Night*

6. The episode of Francesca and Paolo is found in
[A] the Inferno   [B] Limbo   [C] Purgatory   [D] Heaven
[E] The Elysian Fields

7. "An Occurrence at Owl Creek Bridge" is a story from
[A] *Mixed Company*   [B] *The Lottery*
[C] *In the Midst of Life*   [D] *A Tree of Night*
[E] *The Same Door*

8. James Joyce's volume of short stories is called
[A] *Ulysses* [B] *Dubliners* [C] *Exiles*
[D] *H. C. Earwicker* [E] *The Dead*

9. The story "Melanctha" appears in the book
[A] *The Tree of Night* [B] *Dubliners* [C] *Three Lives*
[D] *Trial Balance* [E] *The Hills Beyond*

10. Francis Thompson wrote
[A] "Ash Wednesday" [B] "The Blessed Damozel"
[C] "The Hound of Heaven" [D] "A Psalm of Life"
[E] "Invictus"

46. Characters in the Novel

1. The Charles Dickens character who always expects something to "turn up" is
[A] Fagin [B] Uriah Heep [C] Little Dorrit
[D] Mr. Micawber [E] Mr. Snodgrass

2. Jean-Christophe's friend was
[A] Julien [B] Lafcadio [C] Eugène [D] Olivier
[E] François

3. The "Okies" appear in a novel by
[A] William Faulkner [B] John Steinbeck
[C] Nathaniel Hawthorne [D] Taylor Caldwell
[E] Harper Lee

4. Pinkie's girl in *Brighton Rock* by Graham Greene is
[A] Mary [B] Rose [C] Betty [D] Emma [E] Tess

5. Mr. Pickwick's faithful servant was
[A] The Artful Dodger [B] Uriah Heep [C] Pip
[D] Sam Weller [E] Charles Darnay

6. Anna Karenina and Emma Bovary
   [A] were cousins   [B] were spinsters
   [C] had many children   [D] entered a convent
   [E] committed suicide

7. In *Pride and Prejudice*, by Jane Austen, the Bennet girl who
   married Mr. Wickham is
   [A] Jane   [B] Elizabeth   [C] Lydia   [D] Mary   [E] Kitty

8. In *The Old Wives' Tale* by Arnold Bennett
   [A] Constance and Sophia travel   [B] Constance elopes
   [C] Sophia goes to Paris   [D] Constance goes to London
   [E] Both sisters remain at home

9. Rosa Dartle appears in Charles Dickens' novel
   [A] *Bleak House*   [B] *Great Expectations*
   [C] *David Copperfield*   [D] *Oliver Twist*
   [E] *Pickwick Papers*

10. The Charles Dickens character who works for Murdstone
    and Grimby is
    [A] Pip   [B] Oliver   [C] David   [D] Tiny Tim
    [E] Barkis

47. Adventure

1. A ship which appears in *Moby Dick* by Herman Melville is
   the
   [A] *Bounty*   [B] *Hispaniola*   [C] *Rachel*   [D] *Argo*
   [E] *Reluctant*

2. The action of *The Three Musketeers* by Alexandre Dumas
   père takes place during the reign of
   [A] Henri IV   [B] Louis IX   [C] Louis XIV
   [D] Louis XIII   [E] Francis I

3. *The Innocent Voyage* by Richard Hughes is also published as
   [A] *Tom Sawyer*   [B] *The Lord of the Flies*
   [C] *A High Wind in Jamaica*   [D] *Treasure Island*
   [E] *Oliver Twist*

4. Barnaby Conrad has written an encyclopedia of
   [A] racing   [B] boxing   [C] hunting   [D] bullfighting
   [E] fishing

5. The tattooed harpooner in *Moby Dick* by Herman Melville
   is
   [A] Tashtego   [B] Daggoo   [C] Queequeg   [D] Ahab
   [E] Ishmael

6. A book concerned with Easter Island is
   [A] *Omoo*   [B] *Mutiny on the Bounty*
   [C] *Treasure Island*   [D] *Typee*   [E] *Aku-Aku*

7. The creator of Mike Hammer is
   [A] Graham Greene   [B] Raymond Chandler
   [C] Mickey Spillane   [D] Ian Fleming
   [E] Ngaio Marsh

8. Nellie Forbush appears in
   [A] *The Citadel*   [B] *Not as a Stranger*
   [C] *Tales of the South Pacific*   [D] *Major Barbara*
   [E] *Jane Eyre*

9. *The Caine Mutiny* by Herman Wouk is a novel about a
   [A] schooner   [B] flotilla   [C] minesweeper
   [D] submarine   [E] battleship

10. Captain Nemo was the commander of the
    [A] *Bounty*   [B] *Pequod*   [C] *Nautilus*   [D] *Argo*
    [E] *Hispaniola*

48. Non-fiction

1. Edna Ferber's autobiography is called
   [A] *A Backward Glance* [B] *A Child of the Century*
   [C] *A Kind of Magic* [D] *The Summing Up*
   [E] *Safe Conduct*

2. The term "momism" appeared in the book
   [A] *The Golden Bowl* [B] *The Silver Cord*
   [C] *Generation of Vipers* [D] *Mosquitoes* [E] *Persuasion*

3. André Maurois has written a biography of
   [A] Harvey [B] Lister [C] John Reed
   [D] Alexander Fleming [E] Dr. Schweitzer

4. The author of *Democratic Vistas* is
   [A] Ralph Waldo Emerson [B] Henry David Thoreau
   [C] Robert Lowell [D] Jonathan Edwards
   [E] Walt Whitman

5. One volume of Sean O'Casey's autobiography is entitled
   [A] *Arrow in the Blue* [B] *Pictures in the Hallway*
   [C] *The Solitary Singer* [D] *A Son of the Middle Border*
   [E] *Toward Freedom*

6. The author of *Seven Pillars of Wisdom* is
   [A] John Ruskin [B] Peter O'Toole [C] D. H. Lawrence
   [D] T. E. Lawrence [E] Lawrence Durrell

7. *Dance to the Piper* is the autobiography of
   [A] Carol Haney [B] Isadora Duncan [C] Agnes de Mille
   [D] Margot Fonteyn [E] Pavlova

8. The author of *The Presidential Papers* is
   [A] Irwin Shaw [B] Herman Wouk [C] John Updike
   [D] Norman Mailer [E] James B. Conant

9. *The Bicycle Rider in Beverly Hills* is the autobiography of
[A] Moss Hart [B] F. Scott Fitzgerald
[C] William Saroyan [D] Robinson Jeffers
[E] Henry Miller

10. Two famous diarists of the seventeenth century are Samuel Pepys and
[A] Robert Burton [B] Sir Thomas Browne
[C] George Fox [D] John Evelyn [E] Andrew Marvell

49. Husbands and Wives

1. The Bennet girl who married Mr. Darcy is
[A] Kitty [B] Lydia [C] Elizabeth [D] Jane [E] Mary

2. In *Julius Caesar*, the wife of Caesar is
[A] Portia [B] Calpurnia [C] Charmian [D] Volumnia
[E] Valeria

3. In Tolstoy's *War and Peace* Pierre marries
[A] Anna [B] Kitty [C] Lisa [D] Natasha [E] Marya

4. The husband of Andromache was
[A] Ajax [B] Priam [C] Hector [D] Theseus
[E] Perseus

5. The man who sold his wife in *The Mayor of Casterbridge* by Thomas Hardy is
[A] Clym Yeobright [B] Michael Henchard
[C] Angel Clare [D] Jude [E] Wildeve

6. Jude the Obscure marries
[A] Tess [B] Eustacia [C] Sue [D] Arabella [E] Susan

7. Becky Sharp married
[A] George Osborne [B] Rawdon Crawley
[C] William Dobbin [D] Lord Steyne [E] Joseph Sedley

8. In *Portrait of a Lady*, by Henry James, Isabel Archer married
[A] Ralph Touchett   [B] Lord Warburton
[C] Caspar Goodwood   [D] Gilbert Osmond
[E] Lambert Strether

9. The girl whom Lord Jim married was called
[A] Mildred   [B] Pearl   [C] Sadie   [D] Jewel   [E] Diana

10. Martin Arrowsmith's wife was
[A] Carol   [B] Leora   [C] Nicole   [D] Hester   [E] Katrina

part two

Compatibility

For each of the questions in this part, select from the list on the right the answer that best matches the entry on the left.

1. The Animal Kingdom. Match the work with its author.

1. *Black Beauty*
2. *Rhinoceros*
3. *The Red Pony*
4. *The Yearling*
5. *Bambi*
6. *The Wings of the Dove*
7. *Pale Horse, Pale Rider*
8. *The Call of the Wild*
9. *The Leopard*
10. *The Fox in the Attic*

A. Eugène Ionesco
B. Katherine Anne Porter
C. Henry James
D. Kenneth Grahame
E. Anna Sewell
F. Felix Salten
G. John Steinbeck
H. Giuseppe di Lampedusa
I. Marjorie Kinnan Rawlings
J. Richard Hughes
K. Jack London

2. Fictional Detectives. Match the detective with his creator.

1.	Perry Mason	A.	Georges Simenon
2.	Charlie Chan	B.	Marjorie Allingham
3.	Hercule Poirot	C.	G. K. Chesterton
4.	Philo Vance	D.	Earl Derr Biggers
5.	Philip Marlowe	E.	Agatha Christie
6.	Inspector Maigret	F.	Raymond Chandler
7.	Lord Peter Wimsey	G.	S. S. Van Dine
8.	Father Brown	H.	John Dickson Carr
9.	Inspector Appleby	I.	Erle Stanley Gardner
10.	Mr. Campion	J.	Dorothy Sayers
		K.	Michael Innes

3. Machinations. Match the literary term with its meaning.

1. An improvised comedy (Italian)
2. A novel in which the central character is a wandering rogue
3. European books printed prior to 1501
4. A comedy in which the author endows each character with some oddity or affectation, some exaggeration of manner, speech or dress
5. A literary style that is characterized by ornate elegance and over-refined speech

A. Burlesque
B. Gongorismo
C. Picaresque
D. Commedia dell' arte
E. Incunabula
F. Comedy of humours

4. Utopias. Match the work with its author.

1. *A Modern Utopia*
2. *Erewhon*
3. *Shangri-La*
4. *Utopia*
5. *Looking Backward*
6. *News from Nowhere*

A. Francis Bacon
B. George Orwell
C. Sir Thomas More
D. Edward Bellamy
E. H. G. Wells
F. Aldous Huxley

7. *The New Atlantis*   G. William Morris
8. *Pala*   H. James Hilton
   I. Samuel Butler

5. For the Birds. Match the work with its author.

1. *To Kill a Mockingbird*   A. Aristophanes
2. *Penguin Island*   B. Harper Lee
3. *The Sea Gull*   C. Anton Chekhov
4. *The Bluebird*   D. Anatole France
5. *Pigeon Feathers*   E. Maurice Maeterlinck
6. *Episode of Sparrows*   F. Ambrose Bierce
7. *Too Late the Phalarope*   G. Alan Paton
8. "An Occurrence at Owl Creek Bridge"   H. Ethel Waters
9. *The Eagles Gather*   I. Rumer Godden
10. *His Eye Is on the Sparrow*   J. John Updike
   K. Taylor Caldwell

6. Personae. Match the character with his or her creator.

1. Becky Sharp   A. F. Scott Fitzgerald
2. Becky Thatcher   B. Kingsley Amis
3. Hester Prynne   C. John O'Hara
4. Mildred Rogers   D. William Makepeace Thackeray
5. Hedda Gabler   E. Mark Twain
6. Eustacia Vye   F. W. Somerset Maugham
7. Emma Bovary   G. Nathaniel Hawthorne
8. Elizabeth Appleton   H. Jane Austen
9. Lucky Jim   I. Thomas Hardy
10. Nicole Diver   J. Henrik Ibsen
   K. Gustave Flaubert

7. People and Places. Match the locations with the people associated with them.

1. Tara   A. Ichabod Crane
2. Sleepy Hollow   B. Hamlet

3. Egdon Heath   c. Scarlett O'Hara
4. Miss Pinkerton's School   d. Mr. Rochester
5. Elsinore   e. Rebecca
6. Rosings   f. Clym Yeobright
7. Netherby Hall   g. Lady Catherine de Bourgh
8. Thornfield Manor   h. The Bennet Family
9. Netherfield Park   i. Becky Sharp
10. Catfish Row   j. Porgy and Bess
                                k. Lochinvar

8. Locale. Match the place with the poet.

1. Northampton Asylum   a. Alfred Lord Tennyson
2. Locksley Hall   b. Oscar Wilde
3. Reading Gaol   c. John Clare
4. Frederick town   d. Samuel Taylor Coleridge
5. Tintern Abbey   e. Dante Gabriel Rossetti
6. Hamelin town   f. William Butler Yeats
7. Xanadu   g. Matthew Arnold
8. Dover Beach   h. John Greenleaf Whittier
9. Moulmein Pagoda   i. Rudyard Kipling
10. Lake Isle of Innisfree   j. William Wordsworth
                                k. Robert Browning

9. Part of the Whole. Match the work with the series in which it appears.

1. "The Knight's Tale"   a. *Canterbury Tales*
2. *The Passing of Arthur*   b. *The Lord of the Rings*
3. *Within a Budding Grove*   c. *Idylls of the King*
4. "John Hancock Otis"   d. *Joseph and His Brothers*
5. "What the Thunder Said"   e. *The Waste Land*
6. *The Two Towers*   f. *Leatherstocking Tales*
7. *1919*   g. *Remembrance of Things Past*
8. *Gospel of the Brothers   h. *Back to Methuselah*
   Barnabas* (play)   i. *U.S.A.*
9. *The Homecoming* (play)   j. *Spoon River Anthology*
10. *The Deerslayer*   k. *Mourning Becomes Electra*

10. Have a Heart. Match the work with its author.

1. *The Heart of Midlothian*	A. Elizabeth Bowen
2. *Death of the Heart*	B. Joseph Conrad
3. *The Heart of Darkness*	C. Carson McCullers
4. *The Heart Is a Lonely Hunter*	D. Cornelia Otis Skinner
5. *Miss Lonelyhearts*	and Emily Kimbrough
6. *The Heart of the Matter*	E. Harry T. Moore
7. "The Tell-Tale Heart"	F. Henry James
8. *Our Hearts Were Young and Gay*	G. G. B. Shaw
9. *The Intelligent Heart*	H. Nathanael West
10. *Heartbreak House*	I. Graham Greene
	J. Sir Walter Scott
	K. Edgar Allan Poe

11. Divine Romans. Match the gods with their attributes.

1. The goddess of beauty	A. Mars
2. The god of speed	B. Diana
3. The goddess of wisdom	C. Venus
4. The god of the sea	D. Mercury
5. The king of the gods	E. Neptune
6. The goddess of the hearth	F. Pluto
7. The goddess of the hunt and the moonlight	G. Minerva
8. The god of fire	H. Vulcan
9. The queen of the gods	I. Vesta
10. The god of war	J. Jupiter
	K. Juno

12. Heaven and Hell. Match the work with its author.

1. *East of Eden*	A. Grace Metalious
2. *Heaven's My Destination*	B. John Milton
3. *The Marriage of Heaven and Hell*	C. F. Scott Fitzgerald
4. "The Hound of Heaven"	D. William Blake
5. *A Season in Hell*	E. John Steinbeck
6. "General William Booth Enters Into Heaven"	F. Thornton Wilder
	G. Francis Thompson

7. *All This and Heaven Too*   H. Arthur Rimbaud
8. *No Adam in Eden*   I. Herman Wouk
9. *This Side of Paradise*   J. Rachel Field
10. *Paradise Lost*   K. Vachel Lindsay

13. Italian Literature. Match the work with its author.

1. *Jerusalem Delivered*   A. Dante
2. *De Monarchio*   B. Niccolò Machiavelli
3. *The Decameron*   C. Carlo Goldoni
4. *The Prince*   D. Giuseppe di Lampedusa
5. *The Leopard*   E. Boccaccio
6. *The Fan*   F. Torquato Tasso
7. *The Betrothed*   G. Francesco Petrarca
8. *Orlando Furioso*   H. Ludovico Ariosto
9. *The Conformist*   I. Luigi Pirandello
10. *Six Characters in Search of an* J. Alberto Moravia
    Author   K. Alessandro Manzoni

14. Who's Who. Match the title with the character.

1. "The Man Without a Country"   A. Dr. Primrose
2. *The Would-be Gentleman*   B. Prince Myshkin
3. *The Stranger* (Camus)   C. Wamba
4. *The Vicar of Wakefield*   D. M. Jourdain
5. *The Merchant of Venice*   E. Antonio
6. *The Egoist*   F. Edmond Dantès
7. *The Count of Monte Cristo*   G. Meursault
8. *The Idiot*   H. Wolf Larsen
9. *The Man of Destiny*   I. Napoleon
10. *The Sea Wolf*   J. Sir Willoughby
                                       Patterne
                                    K. Philip Nolan

15. The Older Generation. Match the children with their parents.

1. The father of Ophelia   A. Isaac of York
2. The father of Jessica   B. Ase

3. The parents of Oedipus   C. Peleus and Thetis
4. The father of Telemachus   D. Shylock
5. The mother of Orestes   E. Polonius
6. The mother of Hiawatha   F. Clytemnestra
7. The parents of Achilles   G. Prospero
8. The father of Edgar   H. Laius and Jocasta
9. The father of Rebecca (*Ivanhoe*)   I. Gloucester
10. The mother of Peer Gynt   J. Wenonah
    K. Odysseus (Ulysses)

16. Epistolary Literature. Match the work with its author.

1. *The Screwtape Letters*   A. Mark Twain
2. *Pamela*   B. C. S. Lewis
3. *La Nouvelle Héloïse*   C. Jean Jacques Rousseau
4. *The Ides of March*   D. Thornton Wilder
5. *The Sorrows of Young Werther*   E. Samuel Richardson
    F. Goethe

17. Home Sweet Home. Match the home with the author who lived there.

1. Sunnyside   A. Charles Lamb
2. Abbotsford   B. Sir Walter Scott
3. Strawberry Hill   C. The Brontës
4. Lamb House   D. Henry James
5. Haworth Parsonage   E. Washington Irving
    F. Horace Walpole

18. Mothers. Match the mother with the work in which she appears.

1. Mrs. Alving   A. *Oh Dad, Poor Dad; Mamma's*
2. Mrs. Bennet   *Hung You in the Closet and I'm*
3. Mrs. Yeobright   *Feeling So Sad*
4. Madame Rosepettle   B. *Ghosts*
5. Mrs. Morel   C. *The Grapes of Wrath*

6. Mrs. Pontifex   D. *She Stoops to Conquer*
7. Mrs. Compson   E. *The Way of all Flesh*
8. Mrs. March   F. *Pride and Prejudice*
9. Mrs. Hardcastle   G. *Sons and Lovers*
10. Mrs. Joad   H. *Little Women*
    I. *The Sound and the Fury*
    J. *The Return of the Native*
    K. *Suddenly Last Summer*

19. Doctors and Medicine. Match the work with its author.

1. *Elsie Venner*   A. Sinclair Lewis
2. *Not As a Stranger*   B. H. G. Wells
3. *The Citadel*   C. A. J. Cronin
4. *Arrowsmith*   D. Morton Thompson
5. *The Doctor's Dilemma*   E. G. B. Shaw
    F. Oliver Wendell Holmes

20. Nominal Titles. Match the work with its author.

1. *Orlando*   A. George Eliot
2. *Tonio Kröger*   B. Thomas Mann
3. *Daisy Miller*   C. Voltaire
4. *Dodsworth*   D. Charles Dickens
5. *Candide*   E. Virginia Woolf
6. *Captain Singleton*   F. James Joyce
7. *Nicholas Nickleby*   G. Daphne du Maurier
8. *Felix Holt*   H. Henry James
9. *Tristram Shandy*   I. Sinclair Lewis
10. *Rebecca*   J. Laurence Sterne
    K. Daniel Defoe

21. Mot Juste. Match the expression with the author associated with it.

1. "portmanteau words"   A. James Joyce
2. "acte gratuit"   B. Marcel Proust

3. "engagement"   c. Jean-Paul Sartre
4. "intermittences of the heart"   d. Lewis Carroll
5. "epiphanies"   e. Charles Dickens
                                   f. André Gide

22. Military and Naval. Match the character with the work in which he appears.

1. Captain Queeg   A. *The Naked and the Dead*
2. Captain Hook   B. *The Caine Mutiny*
3. Captain Ahab   C. *Peter Pan*
4. Sergeant Sam Croft   D. *The Red Badge of Courage*
5. Major Scobie   E. *Mr. Roberts*
6. Ensign Pulver   F. *Moby Dick*
7. Lieutenant Frederick Henry   G. *From Here to Eternity*
8. Henry Fleming   H. *Mutiny on the Bounty*
9. Noah Ackerman   I. *A Farewell to Arms*
10. Private First Class Prewitt J. *The Young Lions*
                                 K. *The Heart of the Matter*

23. Picaresque Novels. Match the work with its author.

1. *Gil Blas*   A. Alain Le Sage
2. *The Satyricon*   B. Henry Fielding
3. *Moll Flanders*   C. Jonathan Swift
4. *Jonathan Wild*   D. Thomas Mann
5. *Confessions of Felix Krull*   E. Daniel Defoe
                                   F. Petronius Arbiter

24. Be It Ever So Humble. Match the place with its name.

1. King Arthur's court   A. Raveloe
2. Jeeter Lester's home   B. Manderlay
3. Mr. Rochester's home   C. Tobacco Road
4. Scarlett O'Hara's home D. Camelot
5. Silas Marner's home   E. Tara
                          F. Thornfield Manor

25. The World of Henry James. Match the character with the work in which he or she appears.

1. Flora
2. Catherine Sloper
3. Lambert Strether
4. Madame Merle
5. Kate Croy

A. *The Golden Bowl*
B. *Portrait of a Lady*
C. *The Turn of the Screw*
D. *The Wings of the Dove*
E. *Washington Square*
F. *The Ambassadors*

26. All That Glitters. Match the work with its author.

1. *The Golden Day*
2. *The Silver Cord*
3. "The Gold Bug"
4. *The Silver Chalice*
5. *The Golden Bough*
6. *The Gold of Troy*
7. *The Man with the Golden Arm*
8. *The Golden Ass*
9. *Golden Boy*
10. *The Silver Box*

A. Edgar Allan Poe
B. Sir James George Frazer
C. Thomas Costain
D. Apuleius
E. Clifford Odets
F. Nelson Algren
G. F. Scott Fitzgerald
H. Robert Payne
I. John Galsworthy
J. Sidney Howard
K. Lewis Mumford

27. "Black." Match the work with its author.

1. *The Black Tulip*
2. *Black Mischief*
3. *The Black Riders*
4. *Black Boy*
5. *The Snow Was Black*
6. *Black Narcissus*
7. *The Black Dwarf*
8. *The Black Book*
9. *Black Spring*
10. *The Black Swan*

A. Richard Wright
B. Evelyn Waugh
C. Alexandre Dumas *père*
D. Georges Simenon
E. Clifford Odets
F. Thomas Mann
G. Stephen Crane
H. Sir Walter Scott
I. Rumer Godden
J. Lawrence Durrell
K. Henry Miller

28. Scene of Action. Match the location with the work.

1. Dublin: June 16, 1904
2. Oceania
3. Sanatorium at Davos
4. Central London Hatchery and Conditioning Centre
5. Clongowes Wood College

A. *Brave New World* (Aldous Huxley)
B. *Ulysses* (James Joyce)
C. *The Magic Mountain* (Thomas Mann)
D. *Vile Bodies* (Evelyn Waugh)
E. *1984* (George Orwell)
F. *Portrait of the Artist as a Young Man* (James Joyce)

29. A Collection. Match the volume of short stories with its author.

1. *A Tree of Night*
2. *The Wide Net*
3. *Dubliners*
4. *Adventures in the Skin Trade*
5. *In the Midst of Life*

A. James Joyce
B. Ambrose Bierce
C. Truman Capote
D. Eudora Welty
E. Dylan Thomas
F. Edith Wharton

30. Biography and Autobiography. Match the work with the author.

1. *Act One*
2. *The Summing Up*
3. *The Seven Storey Mountain*
4. *This I Remember*
5. *Out of My Life and Thought*

A. André Gide
B. W. Somerset Maugham
C. Eleanor Roosevelt
D. Moss Hart
E. Thomas Merton
F. Albert Schweitzer

31. Mirabile Dictu. Match the Latin title with its English author.

1. *Sartor Resartus*
2. "Pulvis et Umbra"
3. *De Profundis*

A. Robert Louis Stevenson
B. George Moore
C. Thomas Carlyle

4. *Apologia pro sua Vita*   D. A. E. Housman
5. *Ave, Salve, Vale*   E. Oscar Wilde
    F. John Henry Newman

32. Brevity. Match the work with its author.

1. *Hérodiade*   A. Alexander Goncharov
2. *Victory*   B. Thomas Mann
3. *Pierre*   C. Malcolm Lowry
4. *Oblomov*   D. Leo Tolstoy
5. *Buddenbrooks*   E. John Milton
6. *Resurrection*   F. Mallarmé
7. *Comus*   G. Joseph Conrad
8. *Thaïs*   H. Anatole France
9. *Romola*   I. Voltaire
10. *Ultramarine*   J. Herman Melville
    K. George Eliot

33. Of Ships. Match the captain with his ship.

1. Captain Bligh   A. The *Indomitable*
2. Captain Traprock   B. The *H.M.S. Pinafore*
3. Captain Larsen   C. *Ghost*
4. Jason   D. *Lydia* or *Sutherland* or
5. Captain Horatio Hornblower   *Atropos*
6. Captain Corcoran   E. The *Bounty*
7. Captain the Honorable   F. The *Kawa*
  Edward Fairfax Vere   G. The *Hispaniola*
8. Captain Smollett   H. The *Lollipop*
    I. *Argo*

34. Itinerary. Match the work with its author.

1. *Down and Out in London and*   A. Glenway Wescott
  Paris   B. Beaumarchais
2. *Woman of Rome*   C. Bertolt Brecht

3. *The Berlin Stories*   D. George Orwell
4. *Barbary Shore*   E. Alberto Moravia
5. *Boston Adventure*   F. Philip Barry
6. *The Gentleman from San*   G. Ivan Bunin
   Francisco   H. Jean Stafford
7. *Incident at Vichy*   I. Arthur Miller
8. *The Barber of Seville*   J. Norman Mailer
9. *The Philadelphia Story*   K. Christopher Isherwood
10. *Apartment in Athens*

35. Essays Famous and Popular. Match the work with its author.

1. *The Myth of Sisyphus*   A. Harry Golden
2. *Only in America*   B. Edmund Wilson
3. *Essays of Elia*   C. Albert Camus
4. *The Liberal Imagination*   D. Virginia Woolf
5. *The Common Reader*   E. Charles Lamb
                                   F. Lionel Trilling

36. North, East, South, West. Match the work with its author.

1. *North to the Orient*   A. Norman Douglas
2. *South Wind*   B. Eugene O'Neill
3. *East of Eden*   C. Kenneth Roberts
4. *Northwest Passage*   D. Helen MacInnes
5. *Westward Ho!*   E. Charles Kingsley
6. *North of Rome*   F. John Steinbeck
7. *East Lynne*   G. Patrick Dennis
8. *All Quiet on the Western Front* H. John O'Hara
9. *Ten North Frederick*   I. Anne Morrow Lindbergh
10. *Bound East for Cardiff*   J. Mrs. Henry Wood
                                   K. Erich Maria Remarque

37. Literary Terms. Match the example or description with its name.

1. *The Pilgrim's Progress*   A. Metathesis
2. Able was I ere I saw Elba (the B. Allegory

same when read forwards or backwards)

3. "Milton! thou shouldst be living at this hour"
4. A poem in the first person revealing a dramatic moment in the life of the speaker
5. A ludicrous blunder in the use of words
6. The act of attributing to an inanimate object feelings that the object does not possess
7. Aristotle's term for the purging of emotions by pity and terror
8. A character through whom an author presents his own ideas and feelings
9. Excessive pride that inevitably receives retribution (Greek tragedy)
10. The method of revealing a character's thoughts as the character speaks his thoughts aloud to himself

C. Mouthpiece, raisonneur
D. Palindrome
E. Hubris (Hybris)
F. Apostrophe
G. Dramatic monologue
H. Soliloquy
I. Pathetic fallacy of personification
J. Malapropism
K. Catharsis

38. The Time Has Come. Match the work with its author.

1. *Burmese Days*
2. *Two Weeks in Another Town*
3. *A Month in the Country*
4. *The Years*
5. *Their Finest Hour*
6. *Seize the Day*
7. *Afternoon Men*
8. *Night Flight*
9. *A Clockwork Orange*
10. *Hard Times*

A. Virginia Woolf
B. Irwin Shaw
C. Antoine de Saint-Exupéry
D. Winston Churchill
E. John Dos Passos
F. Saul Bellow
G. Charles Dickens
H. George Orwell
I. Ivan Turgenev
J. Anthony Burgess
K. Anthony Powell

39. Flowers. Match the work with its author.

1.	*Black Narcissus*	A. Alexandre Dumas *fils*
2.	*Prater Violet*	B. James Thomas Flexner
3.	*The Rose Tattoo*	C. Thomas Costain
4.	*The Lady of the Camellias*	D. Amy Lowell
5.	"Lilacs"	E. Rumer Godden
6.	*The Black Rose*	F. Frances Parkinson Keyes
7.	*Pull My Daisy*	G. Christopher Isherwood
8.	*Blue Camellia*	H. Tennessee Williams
9.	*Peony*	I. Pearl Buck
10.	*The Romaunt of the Rose*	J. Geoffrey Chaucer
		K. Jack Kerouac

40. The B's Have It. Match the work with its author.

1.	*Barabbas*	A. Charles Perrault
2.	*Balthazar* (Novel)	B. Felix Salten
3.	*Bel-Ami*	C. Charles G. Norris
4.	*Ben-Hur*	D. Lord Byron
5.	*Bread*	E. Henrik Ibsen
6.	*Beppo*	F. Eugène Ionesco
7.	*Bambi*	G. Henry Green
8.	*Brand*	H. Pär Lagerkvist
9.	*Bluebeard*	I. General Lew Wallace
10.	*Back*	J. Guy de Maupassant
		K. Lawrence Durrell

41. Epic. Match the epic with its country of origin.

1.	The *Lusiads*	A. Spain
2.	The *Kalevala*	B. Babylon
3.	*Paradise Lost*	C. Portugal
4.	*Gilgamesh*	D. England
5.	*Poema del Cid*	E. Finland
		F. Iceland

42. Bride and Bridegroom. Match the work with its author.

1. *Father of the Bride*	A. Washington Irving
2. *The Bride of Lammermoor*	B. Lord Byron
3. *The Bride of Messina*	C. Johann von Schiller
4. "The Spectre Bridegroom"	D. Percy Bysshe Shelley
5. *The Bride of Abydos*	E. Edward Streeter
	F. Sir Walter Scott

43. His Infernal Majesty. Match the work with its author.

1. "The Devil and Daniel Webster"	A. G. B. Shaw
2. *The Devil's Disciple*	B. Aldous Huxley
3. *The Devil and the Good Lord*	C. Jean-Paul Sartre
4. *The Devils of Loudun*	D. Stephen Vincent Benét
5. *The Devil's Dictionary*	E. Henry Miller
6. *The Devil's Advocate*	F. Christopher Marlowe
7. *Devil Water*	G. Morris West
8. *A Devil in Paradise*	H. Raymond Radiguet
9. *The White Devil*	I. John Webster
10. *Devil in the Flesh*	J. Anya Seton
	K. Ambrose Bierce

44. First Person Singular. Match the work with its author.

1. *I, Claudius*	A. Alfred Duggan
2. *A World I Never Made*	B. A. E. Housman
3. *I Accuse*	C. Robert Graves
4. *As I Lay Dying*	D. Émile Zola
5. *I Am a Camera*	E. Sean O'Casey
6. "I Hear America Singing"	F. William Faulkner
7. "When I was One-and-Twenty"	G. John Van Druten
8. *Ego*	H. James Agate
9. *I Knock at the Door*	I. Alan Seeger
10. *I Have a Rendezvous with Death*	J. Walt Whitman
	K. James T. Farrell

45. Palette and Brush. Match the artist with the work in which he appears.

1. Basil Hallward
2. Charles Strickland
3. Louis Dubedat
4. Gulley Jimson
5. Elstir

A. *The Moon and Sixpence*
B. *Within a Budding Grove* (*Remembrance of Things Past*)
C. *The Woman in White*
D. *The Doctor's Dilemma*
E. *The Picture of Dorian Gray*
F. *The Horse's Mouth*

46. Personal Pronoun "You." Match the work with its author.

1. *You Never Can Tell*
2. *Right You Are If You Think You Are*
3. *You Can't Go Home Again*
4. *"You, Andrew Marvell"*
5. *Thank You, Mr. Moto*
6. *Both Your Houses*
7. *You Know Me, Al*
8. *You Can't Take It With You*

A. Maxwell Anderson
B. Luigi Pirandello
C. Kaufman and Hart
D. Robert Benchley
E. G. B. Shaw
F. Ring Lardner
G. Archibald MacLeish
H. Thomas Wolfe
I. J. P. Marquand

47. Mr., Mrs. and Miss. Match the work with its author.

1. *Miss Lonelyhearts*
2. *Mrs. Dalloway*
3. *Mrs. Wiggs of the Cabbage Patch*
4. *Mr. Midshipman Easy*
5. *Mrs. Miniver*
6. *Miss Lulu Bett*
7. *Mister Johnson*
8. *Mr. Britling Sees It Through*
9. *Mr. Pim Passes By*
10. *Mr. Norris Changes Trains*

A. Christopher Isherwood
B. Joyce Cary
C. Jan Struther
D. A. A. Milne
E. Nathanael West
F. Frederick Marryat
G. Virginia Woolf
H. H. G. Wells
I. Alice Hegan Rice
J. Evelyn Waugh
K. Zona Gale

48. Strange Titles. Match the work with its author.

1. *Nausea*	A. Victor Hugo
2. *7½ cents*	B. Richard Bissell
3. *Either/Or*	C. Philip Wylie
4. *Ninety-three*	D. Stephen Vincent Benét
5. *Catch 22*	E. Joseph Heller
6. *Aku-Aku*	F. Sören Kierkegaard
7. *Thirteen O'Clock*	G. Thor Heyerdahl
8. *Opus 21*	H. James Thurber
9. *Diff'rent*	I. Jean-Paul Sartre
10. *R.U.R.*	J. Eugene O'Neill
	K. Karel Čapek

49. American Novels. Match the character with the work in which he or she appears.

1. Dick Diver	A. *Tobacco Road*
2. Joanna Burden	B. *The Grapes of Wrath*
3. Thea Kronborg	C. *Tender Is the Night*
4. Eugene Gant	D. *Look Homeward, Angel* or *Of Time and the River*
5. Roberta Alden	
6. Jake Barnes	E. *Light in August*
7. Temple Drake	F. *Main Street*
8. Ellie May Lester	G. *An American Tragedy*
9. Carol Kennicott	H. *The Song of the Lark*
10. Tom Joad	I. *Sanctuary*
	J. *Babbitt*
	K. *The Sun Also Rises*

50. Worlds. Match the work with its author.

1. *Way of the World*	A. H. G. Wells
2. *World as Will and Idea*	B. William Congreve
3. *War of the Worlds*	C. Edgar Rice Burroughs
4. *The Lost World*	D. Sinclair Lewis
5. *World Enough and Time*	E. Robert Penn Warren

6. *The Infernal World of Branwell*
   Brontë
7. *The World in the Evening*
8. *World Within World*
9. *World So Wide*
10. *A World I Never Made*

F. Daphne du Maurier
G. Arthur Schopenhauer
H. A. Conan Doyle
I. Christopher Isherwood
J. Stephen Spender
K. James T. Farrell

51. To Sleep. Match the work with its author.

1. "Dream Children"
2. *The American Dream* (play)
3. "The Dream of Gerontius"
4. *Dream Play*
5. *Life Is a Dream*
6. *The Dream of the Rood*
7. *Dream Girl*
8. *The Dream Life of Balso Snell*
9. *The Dreamy Kid*
10. "A Dream of Fair Women"

A. Nathanael West
B. Elmer Rice
C. Pedro Calderón de la
   Barca
D. Alfred Lord Tennyson
E. Charles Lamb
F. August Strindberg
G. William Wordsworth
H. Eugene O'Neill
I. Cynewulf
J. John Henry Newman
K. Edward Albee

52. Months. Match the work with its author.

1. *Now in November*
2. *The Ides of March*
3. *Trouble in July*
4. *Middlemarch*
5. *Seven Days in May*

A. Josephine Johnson
B. Fletcher Knebel and Charles
   Bailey
C. Erskine Caldwell
D. Émile Zola
E. George Eliot
F. Thornton Wilder

53. Tempus Fugit. Match the work with its author.

1. *Time Must Have a Stop*
2. *One Man in His Time*
3. *The Time of Your Life*

A. J. B. Priestley
B. Thornton Wilder
C. Aldous Huxley

4. *Time and the Conways*   D. Henri Bergson
5. *For the Time Being* (poetry)   E. Paul Osborn
6. *The Time Machine*   F. Ellen Glasgow
7. *The Time of Man*   G. W. H. Auden
8. *Time and Free Will*   H. William Saroyan
9. *Time Importuned*   I. Sylvia Townsend Warner
10. *On Borrowed Time*   J. H. G. Wells
                                   K. Elizabeth Madox Roberts

54. Biographies. Match the biography with its subject.

1. Catherine Drinker Bowen's   A. Heinrich Schliemann
   Yankee from Olympus   B. Jack London
2. Carl Sandburg's *The Prairie* C. John Barrymore
   Years   D. Oliver Wendell Holmes
3. Gene Fowler's *Good-night,*   E. F. Scott Fitzgerald
   Sweet Prince   F. Walt Whitman
4. Aileen Pippett's *The Moth and* G. Virginia Woolf
   the Flame   H. Edgar Allan Poe
5. Arthur Mizener's *The Far Side* I. Emily Dickinson
   of Paradise   J. Eugene O'Neill
6. Irving Stone's *Sailor on*   K. Abraham Lincoln
   Horseback
7. Gay Wilson Allen's *The*
   Solitary Singer
8. Hervey Allen's *Israfel*
9. Croswell Bowen's *Curse of the*
   Misbegotten
10. Robert Payne's *The Gold of Troy*

55. Man and God. Match the work with its author.

1. *The Nazarene*   A. Lloyd C. Douglas
2. *Song of Bernadette*   B. Morris West
3. *The Shoes of the Fisherman*   C. Sholem Asch
4. *The Robe*   D. Franz Werfel
5. *The Keys of the Kingdom*   E. Taylor Caldwell
                                  F. A. J. Cronin

56. Money! Money! Money! Match the work with its author.

1. *The Financier*	A. William Dean Howells
2. *A Hazard of New Fortunes*	B. Theodore Dreiser
3. *The Millionairess*	C. Nathanael West
4. *A Cool Million*	D. G. B. Shaw
5. *The Counterfeiters*	E. André Gide
	F. Molière

57. Summum Bonum. Match the work with its author.

1. *On the Nature of Things*	A. Zeno
2. *Consolation of Philosophy*	B. Boethius
3. *Discourse on Method*	C. Friedrich Nietzsche
4. *Language and Myth*	D. Lucretius
5. *Beyond Good and Evil*	E. Ernst Cassirer
	F. Descartes

58. Daily Pursuits. Match the character with his occupation.

1. The Admirable Crichton	A. Painter
2. Cashel Byron	B. Psychiatrist
3. Lucky Jim	C. Grocer
4. Louis Dubedat	D. Teacher
5. Jay Gatsby	E. Lawyer
6. Silas Marner	F. Boxer
7. Sidney Carton	G. Butler
8. Sir Henry Harcourt-Reilly	H. Realtor
9. Arthur Dimmesdale	I. Bootlegger
10. Babbitt	J. Minister
	K. Weaver

59. Autobiographies. Match the work with its author.

1. *Black Boy*	A. Henry James
2. *A Small Boy and Others*	B. Arthur Koestler
3. *The Seven Storey Mountain*	C. Edna Ferber

4. *Arrow in the Blue*   D. Jean Genet
5. *Drums Under the Window*   E. Thomas Merton
6. *A Kind of Magic*   F. Richard Wright
7. *Act One*   G. Helen Keller
8. *The Story of My Life*   H. Simone de Beauvoir
9. *A Backward Glance*   I. Sean O'Casey
10. *Memoirs of a Dutiful Daughter*   J. Edith Wharton
                                          K. Moss Hart

60. Bilingual Olympians. Match the Greek god with his Roman name.

1. Zeus   A. Juno
2. Athena   B. Mercury
3. Hermes   C. Jupiter
4. Poseidon   D. Venus
5. Artemis   E. Diana
6. Aphrodite   F. Lares
7. Hephaestus   G. Vesta
8. Hestia   H. Minerva
9. Ares   I. Vulcan
10. Hera   J. Mars
                  K. Neptune

61. Literary Span. Match the work with its author.

1. *A View from the Bridge*   A. Thomas Hood
2. *The Bridge of San Luis Rey*   B. Hart Crane
3. *The Bridge* (Poem)   C. William Wordsworth
4. *Waterloo Bridge*   D. Arthur Miller
5. "Upon Westminster Bridge"   E. Robert E. Sherwood
                                    F. Thornton Wilder

62. Address Unknown. Match the location with its creator.

1. Quality Street   A. Margaret Mitchell
2. Sinister Street   B. John O'Hara

3. Joy Street
4. Ten North Frederick
5. New Grub Street
6. 221B Baker Street
7. Green Dolphin Street
8. Peachtree Street
9. Rue Morgue
10. Dulcimer Street

c. Norman Collins
d. Elizabeth Goudge
e. Sir James Barrie
f. George Gissing
g. Graham Greene
h. A. Conan Doyle
i. Edgar Allan Poe
j. Compton Mackenzie
k. Frances Parkinson Keyes

63. From Book to Stage. Match the play or the musical with the work on which it was based.

1. *The Heiress*
2. *A Case of Libel*
3. *The Innocents*
4. *All the Way Home*
5. *Wonderful Town*
6. *Lord Pengo*
7. *I Am a Camera*
8. *Lost in the Stars*
9. *My Fair Lady*
10. *Hello, Dolly*

A. *Cry, the Beloved Country* (Alan Paton)
B. *The Turn of the Screw* (Henry James)
C. *Washington Square* (Henry James)
D. *The Matchmaker* (Thornton Wilder)
E. *Don Quixote* (Cervantes)
F. *Duveen* (S. N. Behrman)
G. *The Berlin Stories* (Christopher Isherwood)
H. *Pygmalion* (G. B. Shaw)
I. *My Sister Eileen* (Ruth McKenney)
J. *My Life in Court* (Louis Nizer)
K. *A Death in the Family* (James Agee)

64. Omega. Match the work with its author.

1. "The Last Ride Together"
2. *The Last Puritan*
3. *The Last Days of Pompeii*
4. *The Last Hurrah*

A. Edwin O'Connor
B. George Santayana
C. Thomas B. Costain
D. Samuel Beckett

5. *The Last Mile*   E. Robert Browning
6. *Krapp's Last Tape*   F. Cleveland Amory
7. *The Last Tycoon*   G. F. Scott Fitzgerald
8. *The Last Love* (novel)   H. Anthony Trollope
9. *The Last Chronicle of Barset* I. John Wexley
10. *The Last Resorts*   J. Edward Bulwer-Lytton
                                 K. Elliot Paul

65. Essays. Match the work with its author.

1. "Dream Children"   A. Henry Thoreau
2. "The American Scholar"   B. John Locke
3. "Civil Disobedience"   C. George Orwell
4. "Such, Such Were the Joys"   D. Ralph Waldo Emerson
5. *Essay Concerning Human*   E. Charles Lamb
   Understanding   F. Kenneth Grahame

66. Crenelations. Match the castle with its creator.

1. The Castle   A. Horace Walpole
2. The Castle of Otranto   B. Rebecca West
3. The Castle of Thunder-ten-   C. Thomas Love Peacock
   tronckh   D. A. J. Cronin
4. Crotchet Castle   E. John Bunyan
5. Castle Rackrent   F. John Buchan
6. Doubting Castle   G. Maria Edgeworth
7. The Court and the Castle   H. Shirley Jackson
8. Castle Gay   I. Voltaire
9. Hatter's Castle   J. Franz Kafka
10. Axel's Castle   K. Edmund Wilson

67. In Vino Veritas. Match the work with its author.

1. *Winesburg, Ohio*   A. Milton Eisenhower
2. *Noon Wine*   B. Edna St. Vincent Millay
3. *Wine From These Grapes*   C. Moses Hadas

4. *Bread and Wine*   D. Sherwood Anderson
5. *The Wine Is Bitter*   E. Katherine Anne Porter
                           F. Ignazio Silone

68. Fictional Teachers. Match the work with its title.

1. a novel by James Hilton
2. a play by Emlyn Williams
3. a novel by Washington Irving
4. a play by Terence Rattigan
5. a novel by Vladimir Nabokov
6. a novel by Sylvia Ashton-Warner
7. a novel by Edward Eggleston
8. a play by Jean Giraudoux
9. a book by Leo Rosten (Leonard Q. Ross)
10. a novel by Charles Dickens

A. *Good-bye, Mr. Chips*
B. *Nicholas Nickleby* or *Hard Times*
C. *Pnin*
D. *Candide*
E. *The Corn Is Green*
F. *Intermezzo*
G. *The Legend of Sleepy Hollow*
H. *The Education of H*Y*M*A*N K*A*P*L*A*N*
I. *The Browning Version*
J. *Spinster*
K. *The Hoosier Schoolmaster*

69. Where the Heart Is. Match the character with the city or town in which he or she lived.

1. George Apley
2. Porgy
3. Studs Lonigan
4. Liza Doolittle
5. Nana
6. Raskolnikov
7. Leopold Bloom
8. Sally Bowles
9. Carol Kennicott
10. Hepzibah Pyncheon

A. Charleston
B. Berlin
C. St. Petersburg
D. London
E. New York
F. Gopher Prairie
G. Boston
H. Salem
I. Paris
J. Dublin
K. Chicago

70. Shaviana. Match the character with the play in which he or she appears.

1. Eugene Marchbanks
2. Henry Higgins
3. Jack Tanner
4. Sir George Crofts
5. Lavinia
6. Ftatateeta
7. Jennifer Dubedat
8. Dick Dudgeon
9. The Dauphin
10. Captain Shotover

A. *Pygmalion*
B. *Androcles and the Lion*
C. *Candida*
D. *The Devil's Disciple*
E. *Caesar and Cleopatra*
F. *Heartbreak House*
G. *The Apple Cart*
H. *Man and Superman*
I. *Saint Joan*
J. *Mrs. Warren's Profession*
K. *The Doctor's Dilemma*

part three

Creeping Ellipsis

1. One, Two, Three. Fill in the blank with the correct number.

1. .... *World* (Wendell Willkie)
2. .... *Pillars of Wisdom* (T. E. Lawrence)
3. ....*Soldiers* (John Dos Passos)
4. .... *Days of Musa Dagh* (Franz Werfel)
5. *The* .... *Steps* (John Buchan)
6. *Soldiers* .... (Rudyard Kipling)
7. .... *Lamps of Architecture* (John Ruskin)
8. .... *against Thebes* (Aeschylus)
9. *Now We Are* .... (A. A. Milne)
10. .... *O'Clock* (Stephen Vincent Benét)

2. Complete the Title

1. *The Moon and* ....
2. *Sense and* ....
3. *Home and* ....
4. *Brewsie and* ....

5. *Man and* ....
6. *Crime and* ....
7. *Sons and* ....
8. *Fathers and* ....
9. *Juno and* ....
10. *Arsenic and* ....

3. Russian Literature. Name the author.

1. *War and Peace*
2. *Eugene Onegin*
3. *Doctor Zhivago*
4. *The Cherry Orchard*
5. *A Hero of Our Time*
6. *Dead Souls*
7. *Oblomov*
8. *A Month in the Country*
9. *Notes from the Underground*
10. *Who Gets the Good Life in Russia?*

4. Shakespearean Heroines. Name the play in which each character appears.

1. Ophelia
2. Rosalind
3. Titania
4. Cordelia
5. Portia
6. Olivia
7. Desdemona
8. Calpurnia
9. Regan
10. Hippolyta

5. The Grim Reaper. Name the author.

1. "Death of the Hired Man"
2. *Death of a Salesman*
3. "The Masque of the Red Death"
4. *The Dance of Death*
5. *The House of the Dead*

6. "The Death of Ivan Ilyich"
7. *La Morte d'Arthur*
8. *A Death in the Family*
9. *Death in the Afternoon*
10. *Death of a Hero*

6. Famous First Lines. Name the poem.

1. "Sweet Auburn, loveliest village of the plain."
2. "Oh, to be in England, now that April's there."
3. "The curfew tolls the knell of parting day."
4. "Much have I travelled in the realms of gold."
5. "I must go down to the seas again, to the lonely sea and the sky."

7. Real People in Fiction. Name the play or novel.

1. Van Gogh (Irving Stone)
2. Gauguin (W. Somerset Maugham)
3. Michelangelo (Irving Stone)
4. Leonardo da Vinci (Dmitri Merejkowski)
5. F. Scott Fitzgerald (Budd Schulberg)
6. Rodin (David Weiss)
7. Emily Dickinson (Susan Glaspell)
8. T. E. Lawrence (Terence Rattigan)
9. Rimbaud (James Ramsey Ullman)
10. Sacco and Vanzetti (Maxwell Anderson)

8. Complete the Pair.

1. Jason and ....
2. Perseus and ....
3. Theseus and ....
4. Daphnis and ....
5. Echo and ....

9. The World of Dickens. Name the novel.

1. The Artful Dodger
2. Arthur Clenham
3. Lucy Manette
4. Silas Wegg
5. Thomas Gradgrind

10. Missing Names. Fill in the blank.

1. "............ Partner" (Bret Harte)
2. *The Mystery of* .... (Charles Dickens)
3. "The Death of ...." (Alfred Lord Tennyson)
4. *The Roman Spring of* .... (Tennessee Williams)
5. *The Ordeal of* .... (George Meredith)

11. One or the Other. Which one wrote the work?

1. *The Three Musketeers* (Dumas the father or Dumas the son?)
2. *The Foxglove Saga* (Evelyn, Alec or Auberon Waugh?)
3. *The Professor* (Charlotte, Emily or Anne Brontë?)
4. *Notes of a Son and Brother* (William or Henry James?)
5. *The Rainbow* (D. H. Lawrence or T. E. Lawrence?)
6. *Eyeless in Gaza* (Aldous Huxley or Julian Huxley?)
7. *The Blue Angel* (Heinrich Mann or Thomas Mann?)
8. *Brighton Rock* (Henry Green or Graham Greene?)
9. *The Octopus* (Charles Norris or Frank Norris?)
10. *Winesburg, Ohio* (Maxwell Anderson or Sherwood Anderson?)

12. Famous Sonnets. Name the author.

1. "Milton! thou shouldst be living at this hour."
2. "When I have fears that I may cease to be."
3. "When to the sessions of sweet silent thought."
4. "I thought once how Theocritus had sung."
5. "Others abide our question. Thou art free."

13. Flights of Poetry. Name the author.

1. "Ode to a Nightingale"
2. "Ode to a Skylark"
3. "The Raven"
4. "The Swallow"
5. "Wild Swans at Coole"

14. Children in Fiction. Name the creator.

1. Kim
2. Tiny Tim
3. Little Pearl
4. Topsy
5. Christopher Robin

15. Royalty and Nobility. Name the author or the work.

1. "My Last Duchess" (author)
2. *The Queen of Spades* (author)
3. *Kings in Exile* (author)
4. Queen Titania
5. Queen Gertrude
6. *The Prince and the Pauper* (author)
7. *The Faerie Queene* (author)
8. *King Lear* (author)
9. *The Count of Monte Cristo* (author)
10. *A Connecticut Yankee in King Arthur's Court* (author)

16. Name the Poem.

1. "Then hate me when thou wilt; if ever, now;
   Now, while the world is bent my deeds to cross"
2. "I wish you weren't quite so deaf—
   I've had to ask you twice!"

3. "It was many and many a year ago,
In a kingdom by the sea."
4. "Dear God! the very houses seem asleep,
And all that mighty heart is lying still"
5. "When I see birches bend to left and right
Across the lines of straighter darker trees"

17. Women in Poetry. Name the author.

1. Pippa
2. Parisina
3. Althea
4. Cynara
5. Silvia

18. Triple Threat. Complete the title.

1. *Gods, Graves and* .... (C. W. Ceram)
2. *Apes, Angels and* .... (William Irvine)
3. *Rats, Lice and* .... (Hans Zinnser)
4. *Space, Time and* .... (Sigfried Giedion)
5. *Men, Women and* .... (Amy Lowell)
6. *Magic, Science and* .... (Bronislaw Malinowski)
7. *Wind, Sand and* .... (Saint-Exupéry)
8. *Bell, Book and* .... (John Van Druten)
9. *Blood, Sweat and* .... (Sir Winston Churchill)
10. *Science, Liberty and* .... (Aldous Huxley)

19. Fictional Pairs. Fill in the blanks.

1. Sherlock Holmes and ....
2. Lennie and ....
3. Lancelot and ....
4. Pelléas and ....
5. Othello and ....
6. Robin Hood and ....
7. Tristan and ....

8. Frederick Henry and ....
9. Fitzwilliam Darcy and ....
10. Sue Bridehead and ....

20. Missing Names. Fill in the blank.

1. ...., *the Weaver of Raveloe*
2. ...., *or Virtue Rewarded*
3. ...., *a Tale of the Christ*
4. ...., *Foretopman*
5. ...., *Esquire*
6. ...., *or the Silver Skates*
7. ...., *or the Modern Prometheus*
8. *The History of* ...., *a Foundling*
9. ...., *the Moor of Venice*
10. ...., *the Story of a Puppet*

21. Literary "Props." Name the work.

1. A bust of Pallas (poem)
2. A comb (short story)
3. A fan (play)
4. A handkerchief (play)
5. An inherited pair of pistols (play)
6. A silver bullet (play)
7. A collection of glass animals (play)
8. A cup of tea and a "madeleine" (novel)
9. A portrait as a mirror for a soul (novel)
10. A riding whip carried by a woman (play)

22. God and Man. Name the author of each play.

1. *Luther*
2. *Salomé*
3. *Port-Royal*
4. *A Man for all Seasons*
5. *The Devil and the Good Lord*

23. Identity. Name the following:

1. The Good Gray Poet
2. The Sage of Concord
3. The Sweet Singer of Michigan
4. The Wasp of Twickenham
5. The French Byron

24. A Writer and His Lady. Name the woman.

1. Dante and ....
2. Boccaccio and ....
3. Petrarch and ....
4. D'Annunzio and ....
5. Abélard and ....

25. Young Heroes. Name the creator.

1. Giton
2. Otto of the Silver Hand
3. Stephen Dedalus
4. Billy Budd
5. Cedric Errol

26. American Plays. Name the author.

1. *Winterset*
2. *Street Scene*
3. *Golden Boy*
4. *Our Town*
5. *Camino Real*

27. First and Last. Name:

1. The sequel to *Sanctuary*
2. First volume of Sir Winston Churchill's *The Second World War*

3. First volume of Will Durant's *The Story of Civilization*
4. Last volume of Dos Passos' trilogy *U.S.A.*
5. Last volume of Lawrence Durrell's *Alexandria Quartet*

28. Memoirs, Biographies and Autobiographies. Fill in the blank.

1. The .... of Casanova
2. The .... of Benvenuto Cellini
3. The .... of Samuel Johnson
4. The .... of Benjamin Franklin
5. The .... of Henry Adams
6. The .... of Jean Jacques Rousseau
7. The .... of the Twelve Caesars
8. The .... of St. Augustine
9. The .... of Alice B. Toklas
10. The .... of Mark Twain (Van Wyck Brooks)

29. The E's Have It. Name the author.

1. Ethan Frome
2. Evan Harrington
3. Enoch Arden
4. Erik Dorn
5. Elmer Gantry
6. Esther Waters
7. Emma
8. Earwicker, H. C.
9. Endymion
10. Ernest Pontifex

30. Books in Series. Name the author.

1. The *Lanny Budd* series
2. The *Joseph and his Brothers* tetralogy
3. The *Yoknapatawpha County* novels
4. The *Leatherstocking Tales*
5. The *Makers and Finders* series
6. The *House of Earth* trilogy

31. Poetry in Flower. Name the author.

1. "The Rhodora"
2. "Lilacs"
3. "The Lotos-Eaters"
4. "To a Fringed Gentian"
5. "When Lilacs Last in the Dooryard Bloom'd"

32. The Animal Kingdom. Name the poet.

1. "What immortal hand or eye
   Could frame thy fearful symmetry?"
2. "Wee sleekit, cow'rin, tim'rous beastie"
3. "A horse! a horse! my kingdom for a horse!"
4. "Thou wast not born for death, immortal bird!"
5. "Tell me what thy lordly name is on the night's Plutonian
   shore?"

33. Two in One. Name the author

1. *Progress and Poverty*
2. *Advise and Consent*
3. *Arrival and Departure*
4. *Hemlock and After*
5. *Strangers and Brothers*
6. *The Power and the Glory*
7. *Puntila and His Man Matti*
8. *Ape and Essence*
9. *Decline and Fall*
10. *The Agony and the Ecstasy*

34. Fallen Angels. Name the creator.

1. Nana
2. Maggie: A Girl of the Streets
3. Moll Flanders
4. Marthe
5. Marguerite Gauthier

35. Lesser-known Novels of Better-known Writers. Name the writers.

1. *The Blithedale Romance*
2. *Redburn*
3. *Villette*
4. *White Fang*
5. *Daniel Deronda*

36. Pairs as Titles. Name the author.

1. *Hero and Leander*
2. *Sohrab and Rustum*
3. *Brewsie and Willie*
4. *Astrophel and Stella*
5. *The Beautiful and Damned*

37. Greece and Rome. Name the author.

1. *Pillar of Iron*
2. *The Mask of Apollo*
3. *Marius the Epicurean*
4. *Family Favorites*
5. *Caligula* (French play)

38. School or Movement. Name the school or movement to which each group belongs.

1. John Trumbull, Joel Barlow, Timothy Dwight
2. Georg Kaiser, Ernst Toller, Kurt Hiller
3. John Donne, George Herbert, Richard Crashaw, Henry Vaughan
4. Lytton Strachey, Virginia Woolf, E. M. Forster
5. Amy Lowell, Richard Aldington, F. S. Flint, Hilda Doolittle, John Gould Fletcher

39. Quotations. Name the source.

1. "I saw Eternity the other night"
2. "Neither a borrower nor a lender be."
3. "Cowards die many times before their death."
4. "that among these are life, liberty and the pursuit of happiness"
5. "I celebrate myself, and sing myself"

40. First Lines. Name the poem or the poet.

1. "April is the cruellest month"
2. "Hence, loathèd Melancholy,
   Of Cerberus and blackest midnight born"
3. "Come live with me and be my Love"
4. "I bring fresh showers for the thirsting flowers"
5. "Up from the meadow rich with corn
   Clear in the cool September morn"

41. Musical Terms in Titles. Name the work.

1. a poem by William Wordsworth
2. a novel by André Gide
3. a novel by Leo Tolstoy
4. a novel by James M. Cain
5. a novel by William Faulkner
6. a poem by Thomas Hood
7. a play by Strindberg
8. a novel by Rosamund Lehmann
9. a novel by Dorothy Baker
10. a play by William Saroyan

42. Spectral Forms. Name the ghost or ghosts in:

1. a play by Kyd
2. a play by Noel Coward

3. a short story by Henry James
4. a story by Daniel Defoe
5. a story by Oscar Wilde

43. Moods and Emotions. Fill in the blanks.

1. *The Anatomy of* .... (Robert Burton)
2. *The* .... *of Young Werther* (Goethe)
3. *Ministry of* .... (Graham Greene)
4. *Ballad of the* .... *Café* (Carson McCullers)
5. *The Edge of* .... (Edwin O'Connor)

44. Literary Regions. Name the author associated with:

1. "Five Towns"
2. "Wessex"
3. "Faubourg St. Germain"
4. "Lilliputia"
5. "Zenith"

45. More Animals. Name the author.

1. *Roan Stallion*
2. *The Red Pony*
3. *The Sea Wolf*
4. *The Animal Kingdom*
5. *Penguin Island*

46. Names. Fill in the blank.

1. .... *Folly* (Joseph Conrad)
2. ...., *Absalom!* (William Faulkner)
3. .... *and Son* (Charles Dickens)
4. *Short Happy Life of* .... (Ernest Hemingway)
5. *The Mask of* .... (Eric Ambler)

47. Murder Most Foul. Name the victim of:

1. Joe Christmas in *Light in August*
2. Clyde Griffiths in *An American Tragedy*
3. Bill Sikes in *Oliver Twist*
4. Meursault in *The Stranger*
5. Tess in *Tess of the D'Urbervilles*

48. Brothers and Sisters. Name the play or novel.

1. Asia, Australia, Europena, and Jimmy (Alice Hegan Rice)
2. Olga, Masha, Irina (Chekhov)
3. Caddy, Benjy, Quentin, Jason (Faulkner)
4. Sebastian, Cordelia, Julia (Evelyn Waugh)
5. Eugene, Ben, Daisy, Helen, Steve, Luke (Thomas Wolfe)

49. Trilogies and Tetralogies. Name the author.

1. *Roads to Freedom* (*Les Chemins de la Liberté*)
2. *The Forsyte Saga*
3. *Joseph and His Brothers*
4. *Studs Lonigan*
5. *Oresteia*
6. *The Lord of the Rings*

50. Cherchez la Femme. Name the woman who completes the trio.

1. Theseus, Hippolytus and ....
2. Leopold Bloom, Blazes Boylan and ....
3. Robert Cohn, Mike Campbell and ....
4. Roger Chillingworth, Arthur Dimmesdale and ....
5. Heathcliff, Edgar Linton and ....

51. The Ages of Man. Name the author.

1. *The Age of Jackson*
2. *The Age of Reason* (18th century)
3. *The Age of Reason* (20th century)
4. *The Age of Longing*
5. *The Age of Anxiety*

52. Twentieth-century English Novels. Name the author.

1. *The Ballad of Peckham Rye*
2. *The Right to an Answer*
3. *Loving*
4. *The Masters*
5. *Brideshead Revisited*

53. Titles from Literature. Give the source of:

1. *For Whom the Bell Tolls* (Ernest Hemingway)
2. *Brief Candles* (Aldous Huxley)
3. *The Little Foxes* (Lillian Hellman)
4. *The Winter of Our Discontent* (John Steinbeck)
5. *The Children's Hour* (Lillian Hellman)

54. Place-names. Fill in the blank.

1. *The Stones of* .... (Mary McCarthy)
2. .... *Haul* (Walter D. Edmonds)
3. .... *Shore* (Norman Mailer)
4. *Decision at* .... (Helen MacInnes)
5. .... *Abbey* (Jane Austen)
6. .... *Revisited* (F. Scott Fitzgerald)
7. *Bound East for* .... (Eugene O'Neill)
8. *The Road to* .... (George Orwell)
9. *The Spoils of* .... (Henry James)
10. .... *Observed* (Mary McCarthy)

55. What's the Weather? Name the author.

1. *The Snows of Kilimanjaro*
2. *The Rains Came*
3. *The Sun Also Rises*
4. *The Stars Turn Red*
5. *The Heat of the Day*
6. *The Wind in the Willows*
7. *The Searching Wind*
8. *Snow-Bound*
9. *A Ripple from the Storm*
10. *Wind, Sand and Stars*

56. Mentors and Teachers. Name the pupil of:

1. Settembrini (*The Magic Mountain*)
2. Cronshaw (*Of Human Bondage*)
3. Lord Henry Wotton (*The Picture of Dorian Gray*)
4. Father Zossima (*The Brothers Karamazov*)
5. Fagin

57. "Green." Name the author.

1. *The Green Years*
2. *Green Mansions*
3. *How Green Was My Valley*
4. *Green Dolphin Street*
5. *The Corn Is Green*

58. Sounds Familiar. Name the author and book suggested by the following phrases.

1. The president of a club touring the English countryside with friends
2. The gradual deterioration of a portrait
3. "Big Brother is watching you"
4. The Legend of the Grand Inquisitor
5. The election of a new Master to a Cambridge college

59. Men and Women. Fill in the blank with "men" or "women."

1. *The Hollow* .... (T. S. Eliot)
2. .... *in Love* (D. H. Lawrence)
3. .... *Against the Sea* (Nordhoff and Hall)
4. .... *of Good Will* (Jules Romains)
5. ...., ..., *and Ghosts* (Amy Lowell)

60. Windy Weather. Name the author.

1. *The Tempest*
2. *Gone With the Wind*
3. *Windswept*
4. *The Grass Is Singing*
5. *Windy McPherson's Son*

61. Good Hunting! Fill in the blank with the correct animal.

1. The Yearling is a ....
2. Buck is a ....
3. Riki-Tiki-Tavi is a ....
4. Bambi is a ....
5. mehitabel is a ....
6. Lassie is a ....
7. Blitzen is a ....
8. Nana is a ....
9. Toto is a ....
10. Rosinante is a ....

62. Volumes of Poetry. Name the author.

1. *Flowers of Evil*
2. *The Tower*
3. *The Rubáiyát*
4. *Bolts of Melody*
5. *Harmonium*

63. Member of the Family. Complete the titles.

1. *The Surgeon's* .... (Sir Walter Scott)
2. *Rappaccini's* .... (Nathaniel Hawthorne)
3. .... *Kisses* (Bruce J. Friedman)
4. *Mother and* .... (Ivy Compton-Burnett)
5. .... *Carrie* (Theodore Dreiser)

64. First Names. Name the author.

1. *Amelia*
2. *Sapho*
3. *Ramona*
4. *Heidi*
5. *Evelina*
6. *Gigi*
7. *Clarissa*
8. *Marnie*
9. *Deirdre*
10. *Justine*

65. Trios. Name the missing man or woman.

1. Blanche Dubois, Stella and ....
2. Constantia Durham, Laetitia Dale and ....
3. Lord Warburton, Caspar Goodwood and ....
4. Léon Dupuis, Rodolphe Boulanger and ....
5. Sue Bridehead, Arabella and ....
6. Gilberte, Albertine and ....
7. Aglaia, Nastasia and ....
8. Mattie Silver, Zeena and ....
9. Fanny Price, Mildred Rogers and ....
10. Brom Bones, Ichabod Crane and ....

66. Men of the Cloth. Name the author.

1. *The Little Minister*
2. *Framley Parsonage*
3. *The Cardinal*
4. *The Vicar of Wakefield*
5. *The Parson's Tale*

67. Shakespearean Characters. Name the play.

1. Bottom
2. Cordelia
3. Bassanio
4. Malvolio
5. Ariel

68. Narrator or Guide. Name the narrator or guide in each work.

1. *Heart of Darkness* (Joseph Conrad)
2. *Moby Dick* (Herman Melville)
3. *The Inferno and Purgatory* (Dante)
4. *Our Town* (Thornton Wilder)
5. *Remembrance of Things Past* (Marcel Proust)

69. To the Ladies. Name the author.

1. "The Lady of Shalott"
2. *The Lady of the Lake*
3. "La Belle Dame sans Merci"
4. "The Lady or the Tiger"
5. *The Lady of the Aroostook*
6. *The Lady from the Sea*
7. *The Old Lady Shows her Medals*
8. "Lady Godiva"
9. *A Lost Lady*
10. *Lady Chatterley's Lover*

70. Same Initials. Complete the name.

1. Lydia L............
2. Roderick R............
3. Alice A............
4. Billy B............
5. Nicholas N............
6. Lucien L............

7. Anthony A............
8. Daniel D............
9. Meg M............
10. Phoebe P...........

71. Star-crossed Lovers. Name the beloved of:

1. Armand Duval
2. Paolo
3. Count Vronsky
4. Robert Jordan
5. Paphnutius

72. Background of War. Name the war.

1. *Homage to Catalonia* (George Orwell)
2. *The Enormous Room*
3. *Brave Men* (Ernie Pyle)
4. *Three Soldiers* (John Dos Passos)
5. *A Stillness at Appomattox* (Bruce Catton)

73. Room for All. Name the author.

1. *A Room with a View*
2. *The Enormous Room*
3. *The Basement Room*
4. *Other Voices, Other Rooms*
5. *The Living Room*

74. Adventures or Adventurers. Fill in the blank with the correct word or name.

1. *Adventures of* .... (Saul Bellow)
2. *Adventures of* .... (Mark Twain)
3. *Adventures in the* .... (Dylan Thomas)
4. *Adventures of* .... (Laurence Sterne)
5. *Adventures of the* .... *in Her Search for God* (G. B. Shaw)

75. Money! Money! Money! Name the author.

1. *The Twelve-Pound Look*
2. *The Gambler*
3. *The Moon and Sixpence*
4. *Three Guineas*
5. *The Threepenny Novel*

76. Alliterative Titles. Name the author.

1. *Rumor and Reflection*
2. *Street Scene*
3. *Summer and Smoke*
4. *The Countess Cathleen*
5. *Progress and Poverty*

77. Big and Little. Name the novel or play.

1. Little Nell
2. Big Brother
3. Little Eppie
4. Big Daddy
5. Little Boy Blue (author)
6. Little Eva
7. *Little Lord Fauntleroy* (author)
8. *La Petite Fadette* (*Little Fadette*) (author)
9. Little Gidding (author or work)

78. "White." Name the author.

1. *The White Deer*
2. *White-Jacket*
3. *The Woman in White*
4. *The White Company*
5. *Poor White*

79. Parents and Sons. Name the son of:

1. Aeneas
2. Bör
3. Ulysses
4. Christine Mannon (*Mourning Becomes Electra*)
5. Anchises
6. Mrs. Alving (*Ghosts*)
7. Mrs. Yeobright (*The Return of the Native*)
8. Gargantua
9. Mrs. Morel (*Sons and Lovers*)
10. Lancelot du Lac

80. Fictional Children. Name the work of literature.

1. Manolin
2. Piggy
3. Maisie
4. Childe Harold (author)
5. Rhoda Penmark
6. Becky Thatcher
7. Holden Caulfield
8. Caddie and Hugh Clavering
9. Miles and Flora
10. Cosette

81. Memoirs. Name the author.

1. *Memoirs of a Midget*
2. *Memoirs of Hecate County*
3. *Memoirs of an Egotist*
4. *Memoirs of a Dutiful Daughter*
5. *Memoirs of a Fox-Hunting Man*

82. "Gray." Name the author.

1. "The Grey Champion"
2. "Lucy Gray"
3. *Agnes Grey*
4. *Grey Eminence*
5. *The Man in the Gray Flannel Suit*

83. What's in a Name? Name:

1. G. B. Shaw's play about Joan of Arc
2. Jean Anouilh's play about Joan of Arc
3. Archibald MacLeish's play about Job
4. Edmond Rostand's play about Napoleon's son
5. Terence Rattigan's play about T. E. Lawrence

84. Epithets. Fill in the blank with the correct epithet.

1. *The .... Jew*
2. *The .... Bassington*
3. *The .... Soldier Schweik*
4. *The .... Crichton*
5. *The .... Ambersons*

85. Caesar, Antony and Cleopatra. Name the author.

1. *Caesar and Cleopatra*
2. *Antony and Cleopatra*
3. *All for Love*
4. *The Young Caesar*
5. *Julius Caesar* (play)

86. Twosome. Name the collaborator.

1. *The Dog Beneath the Skin:* Auden and ....
2. *The Maid's Tragedy:* Beaumont and ....
3. *Stage Door:* Kaufman and ....
4. *The Spectator:* Addison and ....
5. *Seven Days in May:* Fletcher Knebel and ....

87. Decline and Fall. Name the author.

1. *The Fall*
2. *Decline of the West*

3. *Decline and Fall* (novel)
4. *Decline and Fall of the Roman Empire*
5. *The Fall of the House of Usher*

88. The World of Dickens. Name the novel.

1. Dick Swiveller and the Marchioness
2. Bumble and Mrs. Corney
3. Peggotty and Barkis
4. Bella and the Golden Dustman
5. Estella and Miss Havisham

89. Greek Mythology. Name the person.

1. The unheeded prophecies of ....
2. The girdle of ....
3. The wheel of ....
4. The suitors of ....
5. The riddle of the ....

90. Ménages à Trois. Name the woman.

1. Heathcliff, Edgar Linton and ....
2. Angel Clare, Alec and ....
3. Eugene Marchbanks, Rev. Morrell and ....
4. Sidney Carton, Charles Darnay and ....
5. Fyodor, Dimitri and ....
6. Ephraim Cabot, Eben Cabot and ....
7. Michael Campbell, Robert Cohn and ....
8. Damon Wildeve, Clym Yeobright and ....

91. Locus. Name the work in which each appears.

1. Titipu
2. Tara

3. Sleepy Hollow
4. Catfish Row
5. Gopher Prairie
6. Cloud Cuckoo Land
7. Elsinore
8. Ruritania
9. Starkfield, Mass.
10. Shangri-La

92. Doctors. Name the novel or play.

1. Sir Colenso Ridgeon (play by Shaw)
2. Sir Henry Harcourt-Reilly (play by T. S. Eliot)
3. Bernard Rieux (novel by Albert Camus)
4. Richard Diver (novel by F. Scott Fitzgerald)
5. Andrew Manson (novel by A. J. Cronin)

93. In the Family. Name the relationship between:

1. Catherine and Hindley (*Wuthering Heights*)
2. Clifford and Hepzibah (*The House of the Seven Gables*)
3. Hester Prynne and Pearl (*The Scarlet Letter*)
4. Orestes and Electra
5. Constance and Sophia (*The Old Wives' Tale*)
6. Maggie and Tom (*The Mill on the Floss*)
7. Fantine and Cosette (*Les Misérables*)
8. Mr. Rochester and Adela Varens (*Jane Eyre*)
9. Candace and Quentin (*The Sound and the Fury*)

94. Many Moons. Name the author.

1. *The Moon Is Down*
2. *Moon-Calf*
3. *Moon of the Caribbees*
4. *A Moon for the Misbegotten*
5. *The Moonstone*

95. First Person Possessive. Name the author.

1. *My Cousin Rachel*
2. *My Mortal Enemy*
3. *My Heart's in the Highlands*
4. *My Life in Court*
5. *My Son! My Son!*

96. All Kinds of Men. Name the novel in which each appears.

1. Razumov
2. Hans Castorp
3. Winston Smith
4. Augustus Snodgrass
5. Buck Mulligan

97. Peter, Peter. Name the author of the work in which each of the following characters appears:

1. Peter Quint
2. Peter Quince at the Clavier
3. Peter Bell
4. Peter Ibbetson
5. Peter Whiffle

98. Clothes Make the Man. Name the author.

1. *The Overcoat*
2. *The Fancy Dress Party*
3. *The Man in the Gray Flannel Suit*
4. *The Shoes of the Fisherman*
5. *The Green Hat*

99. "Red." Name the author.

1. "The Ransom of Red Chief"
2. *The Red Lily*

3. *Red Roses for Me*
4. *Red Harvest*
5. *The Red Pony*

100. The Children's Corner. Name the author.

1. *Hans Brinker*
2. *The Wizard of Oz*
3. *Uncle Wiggily*
4. *The Goops*
5. *Madeline*

101. The Four Seasons. Fill in the blank with the correct season.

1. .... *Awakening*
2. *The* .... *of Our Discontent*
3. *Early* ....
4. *A* .... *Place*
5. *After Many a* .... *Dies the Swan*
6. *The* .... *Garden* (play)
7. *The Torrents of* ....
8. *A* .... *Tale*
9. *Black* ....
10. .... *and Smoke*

102. Trios. Complete the trio.

1. Cyrano, Christian and ....
2. Grandgousier, Gargantua and ....
3. Mattie, Zeena and ....
4. Hetty Sorrel, Arthur Donnithorne and ....
5. Gabriel Oak, Sergeant Troy and ....

103. Siblings. Name the missing brother or sister.

1. Franny and ....
2. Dorothea and .... Brooke

3. Miles and ....
4. Roderick and .... Usher
5. Tom and .... Tulliver
6. Marianne and .... Dashwood
7. Holden Caulfield and ....
8. Gretchen and .... (*Faust*)
9. Hepzibah and .... Pyncheon
10. Sebastian and .... (Shakespeare)

104. Children to the Fore. Name the title.

1. A novel by Richard Hughes
2. A novel by William Golding
3. A narrative poem by George Crabbe
4. A poem by Robert Browning
5. A novel by Nevil Shute

105. Same Titles, Different Authors. Name the author.

1. (a) *The Human Comedy* (Series of novels)
   (b) *The Human Comedy* (Novel)
2. (a) "The Children's Hour" (Poem)
   (b) *The Children's Hour* (Play)
3. (a) *The Age of Reason* (Pamphlet)
   (b) *The Age of Reason* (Novel)
4. (a) "Death, Be Not Proud" (17th century)
   (b) *Death Be Not Proud* (20th century)

106. Place-names. Fill in the blank with the name of the place.

1. *The Outcasts of* ....
2. *The Murders in the* ....
3. *Appointment in* ....
4. *The Playboy of the* ....

5. *Eyeless in* ....
6. *Christ Stopped at* ....
7. *Timon of* ....
8. *Ruggles of* ....
9. *Two Gentlemen of* ....
10. "The Celebrated Jumping Frog of ...."

107. Astronomical. Name the author.

1. *The Rising of the Moon*
2. *The Stars Look Down*
3. *The Plough and the Stars*
4. *Ring Round the Moon*
5. *No Star Is Lost*

108. M.D.'s and Others. Name the work or author.

1. Dr. Pangloss
2. Dr. Jekyll
3. Astrov
4. Dr. Wayne Hudson
5. *Doctor Zhivago* (author)
6. Dr. Primrose
7. Dr. Rieux
8. Dr. Andrew Manson
9. Sganarelle
10. Dr. Thorndyke

109. Trios. Name the novel or play in which each group appears.

1. Stubb, Starbuck, Queequeg
2. Porthos, Athos, Aramis
3. Olga, Masha, Irina
4. Ephraim, Eben, Abbie
5. Myshkin, Aglaia, Nastasia

110. Titular Locations. Name the author.

1. *Brideshead Revisited*
2. *Tobacco Road*
3. *High Tor*
4. *Quality Street*
5. *A Bell for Adano*
6. *Deephaven*
7. *Woodstock*
8. *Barchester Towers*
9. *Cannery Row*
10. *Howard's End*

111. Mystery and Mysteries. Name the author.

1. *Mysteries of Mithra*
2. *The Mysteries of Paris*
3. *The Mystery of Marie Rogêt*
4. *The Mysteries of Udolpho*
5. *The Mysterious Stranger*

112. Theatre of War. Name the war.

1. *A Farewell to Arms*
2. *The Red Badge of Courage*
3. *The Naked and the Dead*
4. *All Quiet on the Western Front*
5. *War and Peace*

113. Behind the Mask. Give the better-known name.

1. Hector Hugh Munro
2. Ellis Bell
3. François Arouet
4. Diedrich Knickerbocker
5. Sebastian Melmoth
6. Mme Aurore Dupin Dudevant
7. Eric Hugh Blair
8. C. L. Dodgson
9. Henri Beyle
10. Mary Ann (Marian) Evans

Answers

Answers

answers: part one

Freedom of Choice

1. Biographical Matters

1. [D] Abraham Lincoln
2. [B] Bix Beiderbecke
3. [D] a dog
4. [C] Jean Genet
5. [A] Oliver Wendell Holmes

6. [C] Rembrandt
7. [D] *Oscar Wilde*
8. [D] Percy Bysshe Shelley
9. [D] F. Scott Fitzgerald
10. [D] an editor

2. Shakespeare

1. [C] *As You Like It*
2. [E] Petruchio
3. [D] Othello
4. [C] *Macbeth*
5. [E] *Julius Caesar*

6. [B] Hippolyta
7. [D] Cleopatra
8. [D] Titus Andronicus
9. [C] *Macbeth*
10. [D] Malvolio

3. Greeks and Romans

1. [C] Erato
2. [A] Theocritus
3. [D] fire from heaven
4. [E] goat-men
5. [C] Apollo

6. [E] satires
7. [D] Aristotle
8. [C] on love
9. [C] Suetonius
10. [E] the Oresteia trilogy

4. Animals and Nature

1. [c] teddy bear
2. [c] Cerberus
3. [c] an otter
4. [c] an insect
5. [D] *The Voyages of Dr. Dolittle*

6. [D] Argus
7. [B] *Candide*
8. [D] fawn
9. [c] Don Quixote
10. [D] *Green Mansions*

5. Pseudonyms

1. [c] *Miss Sadie Thompson*
2. [c] G. B. Shaw
3. [D] Brom Bones
4. [E] W. S. Gilbert
5. [B] Baroness Orczy

6. [B] Camille
7. [D] Father Madeleine
8. [c] Cedric Errol
9. [D] Richard the Lionhearted
10. [c] George Orwell

6. Omnibuses

1. [E] Samuel Beckett
2. [c] *Remembrance of Things Past*
3. [B] *Four Quartets*
4. [D] The Pentateuch
5. [c] The Apocrypha

6. [c] Pearl Buck
7. [E] Edgar Lee Masters
8. [c] the *Odyssey*
9. [c] *Judgment Day*
10. [c] *The Human Comedy*

7. Which Novel?

1. [c] *Arch of Triumph*
2. [c] *The Scapegoat*
3. [D] *We Have Always Lived in the Castle*
4. [D] *Roots of Heaven*
5. [D] *Lucky Jim*

6. [D] *Youma*
7. [c] *Barchester Towers*
8. [c] *Crotchet Castle*
9. [c] *The Age of Innocence*
10. [c] *Lie Down in Darkness*

8. Poetry

1. [B] "O Captain! My Captain"
2. [B] *Romance of the Rose*

3. [D] "The Rime of the Ancient Mariner"
4. [c] *Evangeline*

5. [D] Thomas Chatterton
6. [C] *A Shropshire Lad*
7. [C] *Aurora Leigh*

8. [D] a sonnet
9. [B] *A Boy's Will*
10. [D] death

9. What's It About?

1. [D] communism
2. [D] the disintegration of a family
3. [D] to bring home Chad Newsome
4. [C] an international plot
5. [B] Faustian

6. [D] Armenians vs. Turks
7. [D] a treatise on education
8. [C] the Argonauts and the Golden Fleece
9. [D] drug addiction
10. [D] ranchers against the railroad

10. Protagonists

1. [C] Joe Lampton
2. [C] Ishmael
3. [C] Irish legend
4. [C] *The Turn of the Screw*
5. [C] Michel

6. [C] Julien Sorel
7. [D] *The Red Badge of Courage*
8. [C] Henry James
9. [C] *Main Street*
10. [C] Edmond Dantès

11. Dramatis Personae

1. [B] *The Importance of Being Earnest*
2. [B] Jude the Obscure
3. [C] *The Castle*
4. [C] Damon Runyon
5. [C] Joe Christmas

6. [E] *The Charterhouse of Parma*
7. [D] G. K. Chesterton and Daniel Defoe
8. [C] *The Young Lions*
9. [D] *The Red and the Black*
10. [D] Marcellus

12. The Children's Bookshelf

1. [D] *The House at Pooh Corner*
2. [C] the Pied Piper of Hamelin
3. [C] *The Last of the Mohicans*
4. [C] Wendy Darling
5. [B] Natty Bumppo

6. [C] *Great Expectations*
7. [D] *Treasure Island*
8. [D] Silas Marner
9. [E] Ichabod Crane
10. [B] Toto

13. Interesting Locales

1. [D] Zenith
2. [D] the Magic Theatre
3. [B] Balbec
4. [C] Hell
5. [D] Egdon Heath

6. [C] a heaven for warriors slain in battle
7. [D] El Dorado
8. [D] Ithaca
9. [C] fire
10. [D] North Africa

14. The Game of Authors

1. [B] Ovid
2. [B] E. B. White
3. [C] Franz Kafka
4. [E] Winston Churchill
5. [C] Daphne du Maurier

6. [D] Jean Genet
7. [D] Pushkin
8. [D] Graham Greene
9. [C] Howard Fast
10. [D] Arnold Toynbee

15. Mythology

1. [B] Andromeda
2. [D] Aphrodite
3. [C] Furies
4. [D] Calypso
5. [C] Penelope

6. [B] the *Odyssey*
7. [B] Creon
8. [D] tragedy
9. [C] Minos
10. [C] Theseus

16. Occupations

1. [B] Chichikov
2. [D] a day dreamer
3. [D] bell ringer
4. [C] historian
5. [B] a mute

6. [D] an architect
7. [D] a boxer
8. [C] a courtesan
9. [C] runs a boarding house
10. [D] a banker

17. Models, Prototypes and Alter Egos

1. [E] Alexander Woollcott
2. [E] the *Aeneid*
3. [C] St. Luke
4. [D] Paul Gauguin
5. [D] *Northanger Abbey*

6. [C] the Holy Grail legend
7. [C] Sinclair Lewis
8. [C] *The Infernal Machine*
9. [C] D. H. Lawrence
10. [D] Hugo von Hofmannsthal

18. Crime and Punishment

1. [B] an Arab
2. [C] Smerdyakov
3. [B] Utterson
4. [C] the Advocate
5. [C] attacking her

6. [C] Milady
7. [E] Hector
8. [C] a moneylender
9. [D] kidnapping
10. [D] Lafcadio

19. Grab-bag

1. [E] wine
2. [B] a musician
3. [B] Cyril Fielding
4. [C] *The Voyage of the Beagle*
5. [C] Jean-Paul Sartre

6. [D] *The Gladiators*
7. [B] Cassandra
8. [D] Thomas Wolfe
9. [D] comedies
10. [C] Tartuffe

20. The World We Live In

1. [D] Fascism in Italy
2. [C] *The Hidden Persuaders*
3. [C] Nihilists
4. [B] Lewis Mumford
5. [D] Marx
6. [D] Rousseau

7. [D] *The Air-Conditioned Nightmare*
8. [C] *The Jungle*
9. [C] *The Theory of the Leisure Class*
10. [B] *Democracy in America*

21. Friends and Lovers

1. [D] Héloïse and Abélard
2. [B] Sibyl Vane
3. [C] *A Farewell to Arms*
4. [C] Elizabeth Barrett and Robert Browning
5. [C] Esther Jack

6. [C] Sophia
7. [C] *Idylls of the King*
8. [C] Léon Dupuis
9. [C] Miss Jessel
10. [B] Vronsky

22. Wars and Weapons

1. [B] World War I
2. [B] Messala
3. [C] the Irish Civil War
4. [C] the *Aeneid*
5. [E] Arthur

6. [C] D-Day
7. [B] *The Charterhouse of Parma*
8. [C] Crimean War
9. [B] *On the Beach*
10. [D] *The Moon Is Down*

23. Kinship

1. [B] Ivanhoe
2. [D] Osbert Sitwell and Edith Sitwell
3. [C] Anastasie and Delphine
4. [C] King Mark
5. [D] Hippolytus
6. [A] Fleance
7. [B] Nana
8. [D] Cordelia
9. [C] Icarus
10. [D] Arthur

24. Literary Terms

1. [C] a mock-epic
2. [C] *The Last Tycoon*
3. [B] *The Ponder Heart*
4. [A] Hollywood and Forest Lawn
5. [B] John Dos Passos
6. [C] series of dramatic monologues
7. [C] masque
8. [D] medieval culture
9. [C] pastoral
10. [C] a saga

25. Religion and Philosophy

1. [D] Ralph Waldo Emerson
2. [D] Nietzsche
3. [E] George Santayana
4. [C] youthful revolt
5. [C] Stoicism
6. [B] Arthur Dimmesdale
7. [E] René Descartes
8. [D] *Lost Horizon*
9. [D] *The Imitation of Christ*
10. [C] *Les Misérables*

26. Where Are We?

1. [D] *The Deserted Village*
2. [B] Ephesus
3. [D] around the world
4. [E] California
5. [B] Pencey
6. [D] Dotheboys Hall
7. [D] Peru
8. [E] India
9. [D] Italy
10. [D] Netherby Hall

27. Novels

1. [C] *Memento Mori*
2. [D] *The Light That Failed*
3. [C] *The Gift*
4. [C] *What Makes Sammy Run?*
5. [B] *On the Road*
6. [D] *Ship of Fools*
7. [C] *The Titan*
8. [C] *The Return of the Native*
9. [D] *Reflections in a Golden Eye*
10. [C] *Tess of the D'Urbervilles*

28. Guess the Author

1. [D] Philip MacDonald
2. [D] Vladimir Nabokov
3. [B] *City of Night*
4. [E] J. D. Salinger
5. [C] André Maurois
6. [A] *Travels with Charley*
7. [C] Nevil Shute
8. [C] Robert Louis Stevenson
9. [D] Robert Graves
10. [C] Richard Hughes

29. The Theatre

1. [D] *Waiting for Godot*
2. [C] Goldoni
3. [D] *The Little Foxes*
4. [C] *Emperor Jones*
5. [C] *Volpone*
6. [D] *Back to Methuselah*
7. [D] *William Tell*
8. [C] *A Raisin in the Sun*
9. [E] *Murder in the Cathedral*
10. [E] *Death of a Salesman*

30. Main Characters

1. [E] Rufus Scott
2. [B] Paul Morel
3. [C] *Darkness at Noon*
4. [A] *Victory*
5. [C] *The Return of the Native*
6. [B] *Mountolive*
7. [D] Lewis Eliot
8. [B] *Dragon's Teeth*
9. [D] James Bond
10. [E] Tom Canty

31. Supporting Figures

1. [D] Dulcinea
2. [D] *The Turn of the Screw*
3. [D] Blazes Boylan
4. [B] *Pride and Prejudice*
5. [C] *Arrowsmith*
6. [D] Olivier
7. [D] *The Devil's Advocate*
8. [D] Esmeralda
9. [D] *Nicholas Nickleby*
10. [C] *Little Women*

32. It's All Relative

1. [C] cousins
2. [C] Lester
3. [C] the Robinson family
4. [C] Hester Prynne
5. [B] Hermia
6. [D] *The Way of All Flesh*
7. [C] Mr. Gant
8. [D] Ivan
9. [E] Dr. Primrose
10. [C] *The Bridge of San Luis Rey*

33. Science Fiction and the Unknown

1. [c] *The War of the Worlds*
2. [d] Thomas Hobbes
3. [c] H. G. Wells
4. [d] Charles Finney
5. [b] *Brave New World*
6. [e] Arthur C. Clarke
7. [e] Ray Bradbury
8. [b] Ruritania
9. [d] Avalon
10. [c] *1984*

34. Places

1. [c] Bly
2. [c] Stonehenge
3. [c] *A Passage to India*
4. [d] *Romola*
5. [d] Death Valley
6. [d] on a cargo ship
7. [d] in a reformatory
8. [c] Netherfield Park
9. [e] Hollywood
10. [b] Tabard Inn

35. Literary Style

1. [e] *Remembrance of Things Past*
2. [c] alliteration
3. [c] gothic
4. [c] *The Ides of March*
5. [c] dactylic hexameter
6. [c] "entertainments"
7. [c] decadents
8. [c] Hap
9. [b] an epistolary novel
10. [c] a Finnish epic

36. Disasters

1. [d] *Hamlet*
2. [d] *The Pilgrim's Progress*
3. [e] bullfighting
4. [d] *The American Way of Death*
5. [c] famine
6. [d] James A. Bishop
7. [d] Mrs. Danvers
8. [d] vulnerable
9. [c] Iphigenia
10. [d] a plague

37. Miscellaneous Writers

1. [b] Ring Lardner
2. [a] John O'Hara
3. [a] *The Myth of Sisyphus*
4. [b] O. Henry
5. [d] Sholokhov
6. [b] Kenneth Roberts
7. [d] Dashiell Hammett
8. [c] Saint-Exupéry
9. [c] Iris Murdoch
10. [c] *Dracula*

38. Myths and Legends

1. [c] water nymphs
2. [c] Pegasus
3. [c] Freya
4. [b] Thyestes
5. [d] Persephone

6. [b] the Cyclopes
7. [e] trident
8. [b] Sisyphus
9. [c] Aeolus
10. [d] Charon

39. Drama

1. [d] *The Ballad of the Sad Café*
2. [c] *Cat on a Hot Tin Roof*
3. [e] *An Enemy of the People*
4. [d] Molière
5. [d] Harold Pinter

6. [d] *A Doll's House*
7. [d] Luigi Pirandello
8. [d] *Curtmantle*
9. [d] Henri Bergson
10. [d] *Heartbreak House*

40. Poets

1. [d] Thomas Chatterton
2. [b] "Adonais"
3. [b] Shelley
4. [b] *Evangeline*
5. [e] John Donne

6. [d] *Lord Weary's Castle*
7. [d] Pre-Raphaelite School
8. [c] "The Hollow Men"
9. [e] Gerard Manley Hopkins
10. [c] Rimbaud

41. Who Wrote . . . ?

1. [b] *Youngblood Hawke*
2. [c] *Annapurna*
3. [d] *Revolt in the Desert*
4. [c] *The Unicorn*
5. [d] *The Bridge over the River Kwai*

6. [d] *1919*
7. [b] *Wickford Point*
8. [d] *Point Counter Point*
9. [c] *Dorothy and Red*
10. [d] *By Love Possessed*

42. Leading Figures

1. [c] Sherlock Holmes
2. [c] Eugene Gant
3. [d] Dr. Gideon Fell
4. [e] Lanny Budd
5. [d] David Balfour

6. [e] *This Side of Paradise*
7. [e] *Of Human Bondage*
8. [c] Willie Stark
9. [d] John Ridd
10. [b] Candide

43. Settings

1. [c] Italy
2. [c] Chicago
3. [c] Carthage
4. [D] Hawaii
5. [D] Amsterdam
6. [D] *Mutiny on the Bounty*
7. [c] Alexandria
8. [D] New York
9. [D] China
10. [c] a sanatorium

44. Professions

1. [D] composer
2. [A] a physician
3. [c] a singer
4. [c] Sancho Panza
5. [c] *Remembrance of Things Past*
6. [D] Mrs. Hudson
7. [c] Jake Barnes
8. [D] a fascist spy
9. [B] a physician
10. [c] a gamekeeper

45. Shorter Works

1. [D] his son
2. [c] *The Courtier*
3. [c] Émile Zola
4. [c] Laura
5. [c] *The Lottery*
6. [A] the Inferno
7. [c] *In the Midst of Life*
8. [B] *Dubliners*
9. [c] *Three Lives*
10. [c] "The Hound of Heaven"

46. Characters in the Novel

1. [D] Mr. Micawber
2. [D] Olivier
3. [B] John Steinbeck
4. [B] Rose
5. [D] Sam Weller
6. [E] committed suicide
7. [c] Lydia
8. [c] Sophia goes to Paris
9. [c] *David Copperfield*
10. [c] David

47. Adventure

1. [c] *Rachel*
2. [D] Louis XIII
3. [c] *A High Wind in Jamaica*
4. [D] bullfighting
5. [c] Queequeg
6. [E] *Aku-Aku*
7. [c] Mickey Spillane
8. [c] *Tales of the South Pacific*
9. [c] minesweeper
10. [c] *Nautilus*

48. Non-fiction

1. [c] *A Kind of Magic*
2. [c] *Generation of Vipers*
3. [d] Alexander Fleming
4. [e] Walt Whitman
5. [b] *Pictures in the Hallway*

6. [d] T. E. Lawrence
7. [c] Agnes de Mille
8. [d] Norman Mailer
9. [c] William Saroyan
10. [d] John Evelyn

49. Husbands and Wives

1. [c] Elizabeth
2. [b] Calpurnia
3. [d] Natasha
4. [c] Hector
5. [b] Michael Henchard

6. [c] Sue *wrong - should be D - Arabella*
7. [b] Rawdon Crawley
8. [d] Gilbert Osmond
9. [d] Jewel
10. [b] Leora

answers: part two

Compatibility

1. The Animal Kingdom

1. [E] Anna Sewell
2. [A] Eugène Ionesco
3. [G] John Steinbeck
4. [I] Marjorie Kinnan Rawlings
5. [F] Felix Salten

6. [C] Henry James
7. [B] Katherine Anne Porter
8. [K] Jack London
9. [H] Giuseppe di Lampedusa
10. [J] Richard Hughes

2. Fictional Detectives

1. [I] Erle Stanley Gardner
2. [D] Earl Derr Biggers
3. [E] Agatha Christie
4. [G] S. S. Van Dine
5. [F] Raymond Chandler

6. [A] Georges Simenon
7. [J] Dorothy Sayers
8. [C] G. K. Chesterton
9. [K] Michael Innes
10. [B] Marjorie Allingham

3. Machinations

1. [D] Commedia dell' arte
2. [C] Picaresque
3. [E] Incunabula
4. [F] Comedy of humours
5. [B] Gongorismo

4. Utopias

1. [E] H. G. Wells
2. [I] Samuel Butler
3. [H] James Hilton
4. [C] Sir Thomas More
5. [D] Edward Bellamy
6. [G] William Morris
7. [A] Francis Bacon
8. [F] Aldous Huxley

5. For the Birds

1. [B] Harper Lee
2. [D] Anatole France
3. [C] Anton Chekhov
4. [E] Maurice Maeterlinck
5. [J] John Updike
6. [I] Rumer Godden
7. [G] Alan Paton
8. [F] Ambrose Bierce
9. [K] Taylor Caldwell
10. [H] Ethel Waters

6. Personae

1. [D] William Makepeace Thackeray
2. [E] Mark Twain
3. [G] Nathaniel Hawthorne
4. [F] W. Somerset Maugham
5. [J] Henrik Ibsen
6. [I] Thomas Hardy
7. [K] Gustave Flaubert
8. [C] John O'Hara
9. [B] Kingsley Amis
10. [A] F. Scott Fitzgerald

7. People and Places

1. [C] Scarlett O'Hara
2. [A] Ichabod Crane
3. [F] Clym Yeobright
4. [I] Becky Sharp
5. [B] Hamlet
6. [G] Lady Catherine de Bourgh
7. [K] Lochinvar
8. [D] Mr. Rochester
9. [H] The Bennet Family
10. [J] Porgy and Bess

8. Locale

1. [C] John Clare
2. [A] Alfred Lord Tennyson
3. [B] Oscar Wilde
4. [H] John Greenleaf Whittier
5. [J] William Wordsworth
6. [K] Robert Browning
7. [D] Samuel Taylor Coleridge
8. [G] Matthew Arnold
9. [I] Rudyard Kipling
10. [F] William Butler Yeats

9. Part of the Whole

1. [A] *Canterbury Tales*
2. [C] *Idylls of the King*
3. [G] *Remembrance of Things Past*
4. [J] *Spoon River Anthology*
5. [E] *The Waste Land*

6. [B] *The Lord of the Rings*
7. [I] *U.S.A.*
8. [H] *Back to Methuselah*
9. [K] *Mourning Becomes Electra*
10. [F] *Leatherstocking Tales*

10. Have a Heart

1. [J] Sir Walter Scott
2. [A] Elizabeth Bowen
3. [B] Joseph Conrad
4. [C] Carson McCullers
5. [H] Nathanael West

6. [I] Graham Greene
7. [K] Edgar Allan Poe
8. [D] Cornelia Otis Skinner and Emily Kimbrough
9. [E] Harry T. Moore
10. [G] G. B. Shaw

11. Divine Romans

1. [C] Venus
2. [D] Mercury
3. [G] Minerva
4. [E] Neptune
5. [J] Jupiter

6. [I] Vesta
7. [B] Diana
8. [H] Vulcan
9. [K] Juno
10. [A] Mars

12. Heaven and Hell

1. [E] John Steinbeck
2. [F] Thornton Wilder
3. [D] William Blake
4. [G] Francis Thompson
5. [H] Arthur Rimbaud

6. [K] Vachel Lindsay
7. [J] Rachel Field
8. [A] Grace Metalious
9. [C] F. Scott Fitzgerald
10. [B] John Milton

13. Italian Literature

1. [F] Torquato Tasso
2. [A] Dante
3. [E] Boccaccio
4. [B] Niccolò Machiavelli
5. [D] Giuseppe di Lampedusa

6. [C] Carlo Goldoni
7. [K] Alessandro Manzoni
8. [H] Ludovico Ariosto
9. [J] Alberto Moravia
10. [I] Luigi Pirandello

14. Who's Who

1. [K] Philip Nolan
2. [D] M. Jourdain
3. [G] Meursault
4. [A] Dr. Primrose
5. [E] Antonio

6. [J] Sir Willoughby Patterne
7. [F] Edmond Dantès
8. [B] Prince Myshkin
9. [I] Napoleon
10. [H] Wolf Larsen

15. The Older Generation

1. [E] Polonius
2. [D] Shylock
3. [H] Laius and Jocasta
4. [K] Odysseus (Ulysses)
5. [F] Clytemnestra

6. [J] Wenonah
7. [C] Peleus and Thetis
8. [I] Gloucester
9. [A] Isaac of York
10. [B] Ase

16. Epistolary Literature

1. [B] C. S. Lewis
2. [E] Samuel Richardson
3. [C] Jean Jacques Rousseau
4. [D] Thornton Wilder
5. [F] Goethe

17. Home Sweet Home

1. [E] Washington Irving
2. [B] Sir Walter Scott
3. [F] Horace Walpole
4. [D] Henry James
5. [C] The Brontës

18. Mothers

1. [B] *Ghosts*
2. [F] *Pride and Prejudice*
3. [J] *The Return of the Native*
4. [A] *Oh Dad, Poor Dad, Mamma's Hung You in the Closet and I'm Feeling So Sad*

5. [G] *Sons and Lovers*
6. [E] *The Way of All Flesh*
7. [I] *The Sound and the Fury*
8. [H] *Little Women*
9. [D] *She Stoops to Conquer*
10. [C] *The Grapes of Wrath*

19. Doctors and Medicine

1. [F] Oliver Wendell Holmes
2. [D] Morton Thompson
3. [C] A. J. Cronin
4. [A] Sinclair Lewis
5. [E] G. B. Shaw

20. Nominal Titles

1. [E] Virginia Woolf
2. [B] Thomas Mann
3. [H] Henry James
4. [I] Sinclair Lewis
5. [C] Voltaire

6. [K] Daniel Defoe
7. [D] Charles Dickens
8. [A] George Eliot
9. [J] Laurence Sterne
10. [G] Daphne du Maurier

21. Mot Juste

1. [D] Lewis Carroll
2. [F] André Gide
3. [C] Jean-Paul Sartre
4. [B] Marcel Proust
5. [A] James Joyce

22. Military and Naval

1. [B] *The Caine Mutiny*
2. [C] *Peter Pan*
3. [F] *Moby Dick*
4. [A] *The Naked and the Dead*
5. [K] *The Heart of the Matter*

6. [E] *Mr. Roberts*
7. [I] *A Farewell to Arms*
8. [D] *The Red Badge of Courage*
9. [J] *The Young Lions*
10. [G] *From Here to Eternity*

23. Picaresque Novels

1. [A] Alain Le Sage
2. [F] Petronius Arbiter
3. [E] Daniel Defoe
4. [B] Henry Fielding
5. [D] Thomas Mann

24. Be It Ever So Humble

1. [D] Camelot
2. [C] Tobacco Road
3. [F] Thornfield Manor
4. [E] Tara
5. [A] Raveloe

25. The World of Henry James

1. [C] *The Turn of the Screw*
2. [E] *Washington Square*
3. [F] *The Ambassadors*
4. [B] *Portrait of a Lady*
5. [D] *The Wings of the Dove*

26. All That Glitters

1. [K] Lewis Mumford
2. [J] Sidney Howard
3. [A] Edgar Allan Poe
4. [C] Thomas Costain
5. [B] Sir James George Frazer
6. [H] Robert Payne
7. [F] Nelson Algren
8. [D] Apuleius
9. [E] Clifford Odets
10. [I] John Galsworthy

27. "Black"

1. [C] Alexandre Dumas *père*
2. [B] Evelyn Waugh
3. [G] Stephen Crane
4. [A] Richard Wright
5. [D] Georges Simenon
6. [I] Rumer Godden
7. [H] Sir Walter Scott
8. [J] Lawrence Durrell
9. [K] Henry Miller
10. [F] Thomas Mann

28. Scene of Action

1. [B] *Ulysses*—James Joyce
2. [E] *1984*—George Orwell
3. [C] *The Magic Mountain*—Thomas Mann
4. [A] *Brave New World*—Aldous Huxley
5. [F] *Portrait of the Artist as a Young Man*—James Joyce

29. A Collection

1. [c] Truman Capote
2. [d] Eudora Welty
3. [a] James Joyce
4. [e] Dylan Thomas
5. [b] Ambrose Bierce

30. Biography and Autobiography

1. [d] Moss Hart
2. [b] W. Somerset Maugham
3. [e] Thomas Merton
4. [c] Eleanor Roosevelt
5. [f] Albert Schweitzer

31. Mirabile Dictu

1. [c] Thomas Carlyle
2. [a] Robert Louis Stevenson
3. [e] Oscar Wilde
4. [f] John Henry Newman
5. [b] George Moore

32. Brevity

1. [f] Mallarmé
2. [g] Joseph Conrad
3. [j] Herman Melville
4. [a] Alexander Goncharov
5. [b] Thomas Mann
6. [d] Leo Tolstoy
7. [e] John Milton
8. [h] Anatole France
9. [k] George Eliot
10. [c] Malcolm Lowry

33. Of Ships

1. [e] The *Bounty*
2. [f] The *Kawa*
3. [c] *Ghost*
4. [i] *Argo*
5. [d] *Lydia* or *Sutherland* or *Atropos*
6. [b] The *H.M.S. Pinafore*
7. [a] The *Indomitable*
8. [g] The *Hispaniola*

34. Itinerary

1. [D] George Orwell
2. [E] Alberto Moravia
3. [K] Christopher Isherwood
4. [J] Norman Mailer
5. [H] Jean Stafford
6. [G] Ivan Bunin
7. [I] Arthur Miller
8. [B] Beaumarchais
9. [F] Philip Barry
10. [A] Glenway Wescott

35. Essays Famous and Popular

1. [C] Albert Camus
2. [A] Harry Golden
3. [E] Charles Lamb
4. [F] Lionel Trilling
5. [D] Virginia Woolf

36. North, East, South, West

1. [I] Anne Morrow Lindbergh
2. [A] Norman Douglas
3. [F] John Steinbeck
4. [C] Kenneth Roberts
5. [E] Charles Kingsley
6. [D] Helen MacInnes
7. [J] Mrs. Henry Wood
8. [K] Erich Maria Remarque
9. [H] John O'Hara
10. [B] Eugene O'Neill

37. Literary Terms

1. [B] Allegory
2. [D] Palindrome
3. [F] Apostrophe
4. [G] Dramatic monologue
5. [J] Malapropism
6. [I] Pathetic fallacy or personification
7. [K] Catharsis
8. [C] Mouthpiece, raisonneur
9. [E] Hubris (Hybris)
10. [H] Soliloquy

38. The Time Has Come

1. [H] George Orwell
2. [B] Irwin Shaw
3. [I] Ivan Turgenev
4. [A] Virginia Woolf
5. [D] Winston Churchill
6. [F] Saul Bellow
7. [K] Anthony Powell
8. [C] Antoine de Saint-Exupéry
9. [J] Anthony Burgess
10. [G] Charles Dickens

39. Flowers

1. [E] Rumer Godden
2. [G] Christopher Isherwood
3. [H] Tennessee Williams
4. [A] Alexandre Dumas *fils*
5. [D] Amy Lowell

6. [C] Thomas Costain
7. [K] Jack Kerouac
8. [F] Frances Parkinson Keyes
9. [I] Pearl Buck
10. [J] Geoffrey Chaucer

40. The B's Have It

1. [H] Pär Lagerkvist
2. [K] Lawrence Durrell
3. [J] Guy de Maupassant
4. [I] General Lew Wallace
5. [C] Charles G. Norris

6. [D] Lord Byron
7. [B] Felix Salten
8. [E] Henrik Ibsen
9. [A] Charles Perrault
10. [G] Henry Green

41. Epic

1. [C] Portugal
2. [E] Finland
3. [D] England
4. [B] Babylon
5. [A] Spain

42. Bride and Bridegroom

1. [E] Edward Streeter
2. [F] Sir Walter Scott
3. [C] Johann von Schiller
4. [A] Washington Irving
5. [B] Lord Byron

43. His Infernal Majesty

1. [D] Stephen Vincent Benét
2. [A] G. B. Shaw
3. [C] Jean-Paul Sartre
4. [B] Aldous Huxley
5. [K] Ambrose Bierce

6. [G] Morris West
7. [J] Anya Seton
8. [E] Henry Miller
9. [I] John Webster
10. [H] Raymond Radiguet

44. First Person Singular

1. [C] Robert Graves
2. [K] James T. Farrell
3. [D] Émile Zola
4. [F] William Faulkner
5. [G] John Van Druten

6. [J] Walt Whitman
7. [B] A. E. Housman
8. [H] James Agate
9. [E] Sean O'Casey
10. [I] Alan Seeger

45. Palette and Brush

1. [E] *The Picture of Dorian Gray*
2. [A] *The Moon and Sixpence*
3. [D] *The Doctor's Dilemma*
4. [F] *The Horse's Mouth*
5. [B] *Within a Budding Grove* (*Remembrance of Things Past*)

46. The Personal Pronoun "You"

1. [E] G. B. Shaw
2. [B] Luigi Pirandello
3. [H] Thomas Wolfe
4. [G] Archibald MacLeish

5. [I] J. P. Marquand
6. [A] Maxwell Anderson
7. [F] Ring Lardner
8. [C] Kaufman and Hart

47. Mr., Mrs. and Miss

1. [E] Nathanael West
2. [G] Virginia Woolf
3. [I] Alice Hegan Rice
4. [F] Frederick Marryat
5. [C] Jan Struther

6. [K] Zona Gale
7. [B] Joyce Cary
8. [H] H. G. Wells
9. [D] A. A. Milne
10. [A] Christopher Isherwood

48. Strange Titles

1. [I] Jean-Paul Sartre
2. [B] Richard Bissell
3. [F] Sören Kierkegaard
4. [A] Victor Hugo
5. [E] Joseph Heller

6. [G] Thor Heyerdahl
7. [D] Stephen Vincent Benét
8. [C] Philip Wylie
9. [J] Eugene O'Neill
10. [K] Karel Čapek

49. American Novels

1. [C] *Tender Is the Night*
2. [E] *Light in August*
3. [H] *The Song of the Lark*
4. [D] *Look Homeward, Angel* or *Of Time and the River*
5. [G] *An American Tragedy*
6. [K] *The Sun Also Rises*
7. [I] *Sanctuary*
8. [A] *Tobacco Road*
9. [F] *Main Street*
10. [B] *The Grapes of Wrath*

50. Worlds

1. [B] William Congreve
2. [G] Arthur Schopenhauer
3. [A] H. G. Wells
4. [H] A. Conan Doyle
5. [E] Robert Penn Warren
6. [F] Daphne du Maurier
7. [I] Christopher Isherwood
8. [J] Stephen Spender
9. [D] Sinclair Lewis
10. [K] James T. Farrell

51. To Sleep

1. [E] Charles Lamb
2. [K] Edward Albee
3. [J] John Henry Newman
4. [F] August Strindberg
5. [C] Pedro Calderón de la Barca
6. [I] Cynewulf
7. [B] Elmer Rice
8. [A] Nathanael West
9. [H] Eugene O'Neill
10. [D] Alfred Lord Tennyson

52. Months

1. [A] Josephine Johnson
2. [F] Thornton Wilder
3. [C] Erskine Caldwell
4. [E] George Eliot
5. [B] Fletcher Knebel and Charles Bailey

53. Tempus Fugit

1. [C] Aldous Huxley
2. [F] Ellen Glasgow
3. [H] William Saroyan
4. [A] J. B. Priestley
5. [G] W. H. Auden
6. [J] H. G. Wells
7. [K] Elizabeth Madox Roberts
8. [D] Henri Bergson
9. [I] Sylvia Townsend Warner
10. [E] Paul Osborn

54. Biographies

1. [D] Oliver Wendell Holmes
2. [K] Abraham Lincoln
3. [C] John Barrymore
4. [G] Virginia Woolf
5. [E] F. Scott Fitzgerald

6. [B] Jack London
7. [F] Walt Whitman
8. [H] Edgar Allan Poe
9. [J] Eugene O'Neill
10. [A] Heinrich Schliemann

55. Man and God

1. [C] Sholem Asch
2. [D] Franz Werfel
3. [B] Morris West
4. [A] Lloyd C. Douglas
5. [F] A. J. Cronin

56. Money! Money! Money!

1. [B] Theodore Dreiser
2. [A] William Dean Howells
3. [D] G. B. Shaw
4. [C] Nathanael West
5. [E] André Gide

57. Summum Bonum

1. [D] Lucretius
2. [B] Boethius
3. [F] Descartes
4. [E] Ernst Cassirer
5. [C] Friedrich Nietzsche

58. Daily Pursuits

1. [G] Butler
2. [F] Boxer
3. [D] Teacher
4. [A] Painter
5. [I] Bootlegger

6. [K] Weaver
7. [E] Lawyer
8. [B] Psychiatrist
9. [J] Minister
10. [H] Realtor

59. Autobiographies

1. [F] Richard Wright
2. [A] Henry James
3. [E] Thomas Merton
4. [B] Arthur Koestler
5. [I] Sean O'Casey

6. [C] Edna Ferber
7. [K] Moss Hart
8. [G] Helen Keller
9. [J] Edith Wharton
10. [H] Simone de Beauvoir

60. Bilingual Olympians

1. [C] Jupiter
2. [H] Minerva
3. [B] Mercury
4. [K] Neptune
5. [E] Diana

6. [D] Venus
7. [I] Vulcan
8. [G] Vesta
9. [J] Mars
10. [A] Juno

61. Literary Span

1. [D] Arthur Miller
2. [F] Thornton Wilder
3. [B] Hart Crane
4. [E] Robert E. Sherwood
5. [C] William Wordsworth

62. Address Unknown

1. [E] Sir James Barrie
2. [J] Compton Mackenzie
3. [K] Frances Parkinson Keyes
4. [B] John O'Hara
5. [F] George Gissing

6. [H] A. Conan Doyle
7. [D] Elizabeth Goudge
8. [A] Margaret Mitchell
9. [I] Edgar Allan Poe
10. [C] Norman Collins

63. From Book to Stage

1. [C] *Washington Square* (Henry James)
2. [J] *My Life in Court* (Louis Nizer)
3. [B] *The Turn of the Screw* (Henry James)
4. [K] *A Death in the Family* (James Agee)
5. [I] *My Sister Eileen* (Ruth McKenney)

6. [F] *Duveen* (S. N. Behrman)
7. [G] *The Berlin Stories* (Christopher Isherwood)
8. [A] *Cry, the Beloved Country* (Alan Paton)
9. [H] *Pygmalion* (G. B. Shaw)
10. [D] *The Matchmaker* (Thornton Wilder)

64. Omega

1. [E] Robert Browning
2. [B] George Santayana
3. [J] Edward Bulwer-Lytton
4. [A] Edwin O'Connor
5. [I] John Wexley

6. [D] Samuel Beckett
7. [G] F. Scott Fitzgerald
8. [C] Thomas B. Costain
9. [H] Anthony Trollope
10. [F] Cleveland Amory

65. Essays

1. [E] Charles Lamb
2. [D] Ralph Waldo Emerson
3. [A] Henry Thoreau
4. [C] George Orwell
5. [B] John Locke

66. Crenelations

1. [J] Franz Kafka
2. [A] Horace Walpole
3. [I] Voltaire
4. [C] Thomas Love Peacock
5. [G] Maria Edgeworth

6. [E] John Bunyan
7. [B] Rebecca West
8. [F] John Buchan
9. [D] A. J. Cronin
10. [K] Edmund Wilson

67. In Vino Veritas

1. [D] Sherwood Anderson
2. [E] Katherine Anne Porter
3. [B] Edna St. Vincent Millay
4. [F] Ignazio Silone
5. [A] Milton Eisenhower

68. Fictional Teachers

1. [A] *Good-bye, Mr. Chips*
2. [E] *The Corn Is Green*
3. [G] *The Legend of Sleepy
   Hollow*
4. [I] *The Browning Version*
5. [C] *Pnin*
6. [J] *Spinster*

7. [K] *The Hoosier Schoolmaster*
8. [F] *Intermezzo*
9. [H] *The Education of
   H*Y*M*A*N
   K*A*P*L*A*N*
10. [B] *Nicholas Nickleby* or
    Hard Times

spearean Heroines

6. *Twelfth Night*
7. *Othello*
8. *Julius Caesar*
9. *King Lear*
10. *Midsummer Night's Dream*

t
u Like It
mmer Night's Dream
ear
erchant of Venice

rim Reaper

t Frost
Miller
Allan Poe
Auden or
Strindberg

5. Fyodor Dostoevsky
6. Leo Tolstoy
7. Sir Thomas Malory
8. James Agee
9. Ernest Hemingway
10. Richard Aldington

s First Lines

Deserted Village" (Oliver Goldsmith)
e Thoughts from Abroad" (Robert Browning)
Written in a Country Churchyard" (Gray)
irst Looking into Chapman's Homer" (Keats)
ever" (John Masefield)

eople in Fiction

Life
on and Sixpence
ony and the Ecstasy
mance of Leonardo da

6. *Naked Came I*
7. *Alison's House*
8. *Ross*
9. *The Day on Fire*
10. *Winterset*

senchanted

te the Pair

neda

us

69. Where the Heart Is

1. [G] Boston
2. [A] Charleston
3. [K] Chicago
4. [D] London
5. [I] Paris

6. [C] St. Petersburg
7. [J] Dublin
8. [B] Berlin
9. [F] Gopher Prairie
10. [H] Salem

70. Shaviana

1. [C] *Candida*
2. [A] *Pygmalion*
3. [H] *Man and Superman*
4. [J] *Mrs. Warren's Profession*
5. [B] *Androcles and the Lion*

6. [E] *Caesar and Cleopatra*
7. [K] *The Doctor's Dilemma*
8. [D] *The Devil's Disciple*
9. [I] *Saint Joan*
10. [F] *Heartbreak House*

Creeping

4. Shake

1. *Haml*
2. *As Yo*
3. *Midsu*
4. *King*
5. *The M*

5. The G

1. Rober
2. Arthu
3. Edgar
4. W. H.
   Augus

6. Famou

1. "The
2. "Hom
3. "Elegy
4. "On F
5. "Sea F

7. Real P

1. *Lust fo*
2. *The M*
3. *The Ag*
4. *The Ro*
   Vinci
5. *The Di*

8. Comple

1. Medea
2. Androm
3. Ariadn
4. Chloe
5. Narciss

1. One, Two, Three

1. *One World*
2. *Seven Pillars of Wisdom*
3. *Three Soldiers*
4. *Forty Days of Musa Dagh*
5. *The Thirty-nine Steps*

2. Complete the Title

1. *The Moon and Sixpence*
2. *Sense and Sensibility*
3. *Home and Beauty*
4. *Brewsie and Willie*
5. *Man and Superman*

3. Russian Literature

1. Leo Tolstoy
2. Alexander Pushkin
3. Boris Pasternak
4. Anton Chekhov
5. Mikhail Lermontov

9. The World of Dickens

1. *Oliver Twist*
2. *Little Dorrit*
3. *A Tale of Two Cities*
4. *Our Mutual Friend*
5. *Hard Times*

10. Missing Names

1. "Tennessee's Partner"
2. *The Mystery of Edwin Drood*
3. "The Death of Oenone"
4. *The Roman Spring of Mrs. Stone*
5. *The Ordeal of Richard Feverel*

11. One or the Other

1. Dumas the father
2. Auberon Waugh
3. Charlotte Brontë
4. Henry James
5. D. H. Lawrence
6. Aldous Huxley
7. Heinrich Mann
8. Graham Greene
9. Frank Norris
10. Sherwood Anderson

12. Famous Sonnets

1. William Wordsworth
2. John Keats
3. Shakespeare
4. Elizabeth Barrett Browning
5. Matthew Arnold

13. Flights of Poetry

1. John Keats
2. Percy Bysshe Shelley
3. Edgar Allan Poe
4. Abraham Cowley
5. William Butler Yeats

14. Children in Fiction

1. Rudyard Kipling
2. Charles Dickens
3. Nathaniel Hawthorne
4. Harriet Beecher Stowe
5. A. A. Milne

15. Royalty and Nobility

1. Robert Browning
2. Alexander Pushkin
3. Alphonse Daudet
4. *Midsummer Night's Dream*
5. *Hamlet*
6. Mark Twain
7. Edmund Spenser
8. Shakespeare
9. Alexandre Dumas père
10. Mark Twain

16. Name the Poem

1. Sonnet XC—Shakespeare
2. "The Walrus and the Carpenter"—Lewis Carroll
3. "Annabel Lee"—Edgar Allan Poe
4. "Upon Westminster Bridge"—William Wordsworth
5. "Birches"—Robert Frost

17. Women in Poetry

1. Robert Browning
2. Lord Byron
3. Richard Lovelace
4. Ernest Dowson
5. Shakespeare

18. Triple Threat

1. *Gods, Graves and Scholars*
2. *Apes, Angels and Victorians*
3. *Rats, Lice and History*
4. *Space, Time and Architecture*
5. *Men, Women and Ghosts*
6. *Magic, Science and Religion*
7. *Wind, Sand and Stars*
8. *Bell, Book and Candle*
9. *Blood, Sweat and Tears*
10. *Science, Liberty and Peace*

19. Fictional Pairs

1. Sherlock Holmes and Dr. Watson
2. Lennie and George
3. Lancelot and Elaine
4. Pelléas and Mélisande
5. Othello and Desdemona
6. Robin Hood and Maid Marian
7. Tristan and Isolde
8. Frederick Henry and Catherine Barkley
9. Fitzwilliam Darcy and Elizabeth Bennet
10. Sue Bridehead and Jude the Obscure (Jude Fawley)

20. Missing Names

1. Silas Marner
2. Pamela
3. Ben-Hur
4. Billy Budd
5. H. M. Pulham
6. Hans Brinker
7. Frankenstein
8. Tom Jones
9. Othello
10. Pinocchio

21. Literary "Props"

1. "The Raven"
2. "The Gift of the Magi"
3. *Lady Windermere's Fan*
4. *Othello*
5. *Hedda Gabler*
6. *Emperor Jones*
7. *The Glass Menagerie*
8. *Swann's Way*
9. *The Picture of Dorian Gray*
10. *Miss Julie*

22. God and Man

1. John Osborne
2. Oscar Wilde
3. Henry de Montherlant
4. Robert Bolt
5. Jean-Paul Sartre

23. Identity

1. Walt Whitman
2. Ralph Waldo Emerson
3. Julia A. Moore
4. Alexander Pope
5. Alfred de Musset

24. A Writer and His Lady

1. Dante and Beatrice
2. Boccaccio and Fiammetta
3. Petrarch and Laura
4. D'Annunzio and Eleanora Duse
5. Abélard and Héloïse

25. Young Heroes

1. Petronius Arbiter
2. Howard Pyle
3. James Joyce
4. Herman Melville
5. Frances Hodgson Burnett

26. American Plays

1. Maxwell Anderson
2. Elmer Rice
3. Clifford Odets
4. Thornton Wilder
5. Tennessee Williams

27. First and Last

1. *Requiem for a Nun*
2. *The Gathering Storm*
3. *Our Oriental Heritage*
4. *The Big Money*
5. *Clea*

28. Memoirs, Biographies and Autobiographies

1. *The Memoirs of Casanova*
2. *The Autobiography of Benvenuto Cellini*
3. *The Life of Samuel Johnson*
4. *The Autobiography of Benjamin Franklin*
5. *The Education of Henry Adams*
6. *The Confessions of Jean Jacques Rousseau*
7. *The Lives of the Twelve Caesars*
8. *The Confessions of St. Augustine*
9. *The Autobiography of Alice B. Toklas*
10. *The Ordeal of Mark Twain*

29. The E's Have It

1. Edith Wharton
2. George Meredith
3. Alfred Lord Tennyson
4. Ben Hecht
5. Sinclair Lewis
6. George Moore
7. Jane Austen
8. James Joyce
9. John Keats
10. Samuel Butler

30. Books in Series

1. Upton Sinclair
2. Thomas Mann
3. William Faulkner
4. James Fenimore Cooper
5. Van Wyck Brooks
6. Pearl Buck

31. Poetry in Flower

1. Ralph Waldo Emerson
2. Amy Lowell
3. Alfred Lord Tennyson
4. William Cullen Bryant
5. Walt Whitman

32. The Animal Kingdom

1. William Blake
2. Robert Burns
3. Shakespeare
4. John Keats
5. Edgar Allan Poe

33. Two in One

1. Henry George
2. Allen Drury
3. Arthur Koestler
4. Angus Wilson
5. C. P. Snow
6. Graham Greene
7. Bertolt Brecht
8. Aldous Huxley
9. Evelyn Waugh
10. Irving Stone

34. Fallen Angels

1. Émile Zola
2. Stephen Crane
3. Daniel Defoe
4. J. K. Huysmans
5. Alexandre Dumas *fils*

35. Lesser-known Novels of Better-known Writers

1. Nathaniel Hawthorne
2. Herman Melville
3. Charlotte Brontë
4. Jack London
5. George Eliot

36. Pairs as Titles

1. Christopher Marlowe
2. Matthew Arnold
3. Gertrude Stein
4. Sir Philip Sidney
5. F. Scott Fitzgerald

37. Greece and Rome

1. Taylor Caldwell
2. Mary Renault
3. Walter Pater
4. Alfred Duggan
5. Albert Camus

38. School or Movement

1. The Hartford Wits
2. Expressionism
3. The Metaphysical Poets
4. The Bloomsbury Group
5. The Imagists

39. Quotations

1. "The World" (Henry Vaughan)
2. *Hamlet* (Shakespeare)
3. *Julius Caesar* (Shakespeare)
4. *Declaration of Independence*
5. "Song of Myself" (Walt Whitman)

40. First Lines

1. "The Waste Land" (T. S. Eliot)
2. "L'Allegro" (John Milton)
3. "The Passionate Shepherd to his Love" (Marlowe)
4. "The Cloud" (Percy Bysshe Shelley)
5. "Barbara Frietchie" (John Greenleaf Whittier)

41. Musical Terms in Titles

1. "The Prelude"
2. *Symphonie Pastorale*
3. *The Kreutzer Sonata*
4. *Serenade*
5. *Requiem for a Nun*
6. "The Song of the Shirt"
7. *The Ghost Sonata*
8. *Invitation to the Waltz*
9. *Trio*
10. *Love's Old Sweet Song*

42. Spectral Forms

1. Andrea in *The Spanish Tragedie*
2. Elvira in *Blithe Spirit*
3. Peter Quint and Miss Jessel in *The Turn of the Screw*
4. Mrs. Veal in *The True Relation of the Apparition of One Mrs. Veal*
5. The Canterville Ghost

43. Moods and Emotions

1. *The Anatomy of Melancholy*
2. *The Sorrows of Young Werther*
3. *The Ministry of Fear*
4. *The Ballad of the Sad Café*
5. *The Edge of Sadness*

44. Literary Regions

1. Arnold Bennett
2. Thomas Hardy
3. Marcel Proust
4. Jonathan Swift
5. Sinclair Lewis

45. More Animals

1. Robinson Jeffers
2. John Steinbeck
3. Jack London
4. Philip Barry
5. Anatole France

46. Names

1. *Almayer's Folly*
2. *Absalom, Absalom!*
3. *Dombey and Son*
4. *Short Happy Life of Francis Macomber*
5. *The Mask of Dimitrios*

47. Murder Most Foul

1. Miss Burden
2. Roberta Alden
3. Nancy
4. An Arab
5. Alec D'Urberville

48. Brothers and Sisters

1. *Mrs. Wiggs of the Cabbage Patch*
2. *The Three Sisters*
3. *The Sound and the Fury*
4. *Brideshead Revisited*
5. *Look Homeward, Angel*

49. Trilogies and Tetralogies

1. Jean-Paul Sartre
2. John Galsworthy
3. Thomas Mann
4. James T. Farrell
5. Aeschylus
6. J. R. R. Tolkien

50. Cherchez la Femme

1. Phaedra
2. Molly Bloom
3. Lady Brett Ashley
4. Hester Prynne
5. Catherine Earnshaw

51. The Ages of Man

1. Arthur Schlesinger, Jr.
2. Thomas Paine
3. Jean-Paul Sartre
4. Arthur Koestler
5. W. H. Auden

52. Twentieth-century English Novels

1. Muriel Spark
2. Anthony Burgess
3. Henry Green
4. C. P. Snow
5. Evelyn Waugh

53. Titles from Literature

1. *Death* (John Donne)
2. *Macbeth* (Shakespeare)
3. "The little foxes, that spoil the vine" (*Song of Solomon*)
4. *Richard III* (Shakespeare)
5. *The Children's Hour* (Longfellow)

54. Place-names

1. *The Stones of Florence*
2. *Rome Haul*
3. *Barbary Shore*
4. *Decision at Delphi*
5. *Northanger Abbey*
6. *Babylon Revisited*
7. *Bound East for Cardiff*
8. *The Road to Wigan Pier*
9. *The Spoils of Poynton*
10. *Venice Observed*

55. What's the Weather?

1. Ernest Hemingway
2. Louis Bromfield
3. Ernest Hemingway
4. Sean O'Casey
5. Elizabeth Bowen
6. Kenneth Grahame
7. Lillian Hellman
8. John Greenleaf Whittier
9. Doris Lessing
10. Antoine de Saint-Exupéry

56. Mentors and Teachers

1. Hans Castorp
2. Philip Carey
3. Dorian Gray
4. Alyosha
5. Oliver Twist

57. "Green"

1. A. J. Cronin
2. W. H. Hudson
3. Richard Llewellyn
4. Elizabeth Goudge
5. Emlyn Williams

58. Sounds Familiar

1. *Pickwick Papers* (Charles Dickens)
2. *The Picture of Dorian Gray* (Oscar Wilde)
3. *1984* (George Orwell)
4. *The Brothers Karamazov* (Fyodor Dostoevsky)
5. *The Masters* (C. P. Snow)

59. Men and Women

1. *The Hollow Men*
2. *Women in Love*
3. *Men Against the Sea*
4. *Men of Good Will*
5. *Men, Women and Ghosts*

60. Windy Weather

1. Shakespeare
2. Margaret Mitchell
3. Mary Ellen Chase
4. Doris Lessing
5. Sherwood Anderson

61. Good Hunting!

1. Fawn
2. Dog
3. Mongoose
4. Deer
5. Cat
6. Dog
7. Reindeer
8. Dog
9. Dog
10. Horse

62. Volumes of Poetry

1. Charles Baudelaire
2. William Butler Yeats
3. Omar Khayyám
4. Emily Dickinson
5. Wallace Stevens

63. Member of the Family

1. *The Surgeon's Daughter*
2. *Rappaccini's Daughter*
3. *A Mother's Kisses*
4. *Mother and Son*
5. *Sister Carrie*

64. First Names

1. Henry Fielding
2. Alphonse Daudet
3. Helen Hunt Jackson
4. Johanna Spyri
5. Frances (Fanny) Burney
6. Colette
7. Samuel Richardson
8. Winston Graham
9. William Butler Yeats or John Millington Synge
10. Lawrence Durrell

65. Trios

1. Stanley Kowalski
2. Willoughby Patterne
3. Isabel Archer
4. Emma Bovary
5. Jude Fawley
6. Marcel
7. Prince Myshkin
8. Ethan Frome
9. Philip Carey
10. Katrina Van Tassel

66. Men of the Cloth

1. Sir James Barrie
2. Anthony Trollope
3. Henry Morton Robinson
4. Oliver Goldsmith
5. Chaucer

67. Shakespearean Characters

1. *A Midsummer Night's Dream*
2. *King Lear*
3. *The Merchant of Venice*
4. *Twelfth Night*
5. *The Tempest*

68. Narrator or Guide

1. Marlow
2. Ishmael
3. Vergil
4. The Stage Manager
5. Marcel

69. To the Ladies

1. Alfred Lord Tennyson
2. Sir Walter Scott
3. John Keats
4. Frank Stockton
5. William Dean Howells

6. Henrik Ibsen
7. Sir James Barrie
8. Alfred Lord Tennyson
9. Willa Cather
10. D. H. Lawrence

70. Same Initials

1. Lydia Languish
2. Roderick Random
3. Alice Adams
4. Billy Budd
5. Nicholas Nickleby

6. Lucien Leuwen
7. Anthony Adverse
8. Daniel Deronda
9. Meg March
10. Phoebe Pyncheon

71. Star-crossed Lovers

1. Marguerite Gauthier (Camille)
2. Francesca
3. Anna Karenina
4. Maria
5. Thaïs

72. Background of War

1. Spanish Civil War
2. World War I
3. World War II
4. World War I
5. American Civil War

73. Room for All

1. E. M. Forster
2. e. e. cummings
3. Graham Greene
4. Truman Capote
5. Graham Greene

74. Adventures or Adventurers

1. *The Adventures of Augie March*
2. *The Adventures of Tom Sawyer*
3. *Adventures in the Skin Trade*
4. *Tristram Shandy*
5. *Adventures of the Black Girl in Her Search for God*

75. Money! Money! Money!

1. Sir James Barrie
2. Fyodor Dostoevsky
3. W. Somerset Maugham
4. Virginia Woolf
5. Bertolt Brecht

76. Alliterative Titles

1. Bernard Berenson
2. Elmer Rice
3. Tennessee Williams
4. William Butler Yeats
5. Henry George

77. Big and Little

1. *The Old Curiosity Shop*
2. *1984*
3. *Silas Marner*
4. *Cat on a Hot Tin Roof*
5. Eugene Field
6. *Uncle Tom's Cabin*
7. Frances Hodgson Burnett
8. George Sand
9. T. S. Eliot (*Four Quartets*)

78. "White"

1. James Thurber
2. Herman Melville
3. Wilkie Collins
4. A. Conan Doyle
5. Sherwood Anderson

79. Parents and Sons

1. Ascanius
2. Odin
3. Telemachus
4. Orin Mannon
5. Aeneas

6. Oswald Alving
7. Clym Yeobright
8. Pantagruel
9. Paul Morel
10. Sir Galahad

80. Fictional Children

1. *The Old Man and the Sea*
2. *Lord of the Flies*
3. *What Maisie Knew*
4. Lord Byron
5. *The Bad Seed*

6. *Tom Sawyer*
7. *Catcher in the Rye*
8. *The Battle of the Villa Fiorita*
9. *The Turn of the Screw*
10. *Les Misérables*

81. Memoirs

1. Walter de la Mare
2. Edmund Wilson
3. Stendhal
4. Simone de Beauvoir
5. Siegfried Sassoon

82. "Gray"

1. Nathaniel Hawthorne
2. William Wordsworth
3. Anne Brontë
4. Aldous Huxley
5. Sloan Wilson

83. What's in a Name?

1. *Saint Joan*
2. *The Lark*
3. *J.B.*
4. *L'Aiglon*
5. *Ross*

84. Epithets

1. *The Wandering Jew* (Eugène Sue)
2. *The Unbearable Bassington* (Saki)
3. *The Good Soldier Schweik* (Jaroslav Hasek)
4. *The Admirable Crichton* (Sir James Barrie)
5. *The Magnificent Ambersons* (Booth Tarkington)

85. Caesar, Antony and Cleopatra

1. G. B. Shaw
2. Shakespeare
3. John Dryden
4. Rex Warner
5. Shakespeare

86. Twosome

1. Auden and Isherwood
2. Beaumont and Fletcher
3. Kaufman and Edna Ferber
4. Addison and Steele
5. Fletcher Knebel and Charles Bailey

87. Decline and Fall

1. Albert Camus
2. Oswald Spengler
3. Evelyn Waugh
4. Edward Gibbon
5. Edgar Allan Poe

88. The World of Dickens

1. *The Old Curiosity Shop*
2. *Oliver Twist*
3. *David Copperfield*
4. *Our Mutual Friend*
5. *Great Expectations*

89. Greek Mythology

1. Cassandra
2. Hippolyta
3. Ixion
4. Penelope
5. Sphinx

90. Ménages à Trois

1. Catherine Earnshaw
2. Tess of the D'Urbervilles
3. Candida
4. Lucie Manette
5. Grushenka
6. Abbie Putnam
7. Lady Brett Ashley
8. Eustacia Vye

91. Locus

1. *The Mikado*
2. *Gone With the Wind*
3. *The Legend of Sleepy Hollow*
4. *Porgy and Bess*
5. *Main Street*
6. *The Birds*
7. *Hamlet*
8. *The Prisoner of Zenda*
9. *Ethan Frome*
10. *Lost Horizon*

92. Doctors

1. *The Doctor's Dilemma*
2. *The Cocktail Party*
3. *The Plague*
4. *Tender Is the Night*
5. *The Citadel*

93. In the Family

1. Sister and brother
2. Brother and sister
3. Mother and daughter
4. Brother and sister
5. Sisters
6. Sister and brother
7. Mother and daughter
8. Guardian and ward
9. Sister and brother

94. Many Moons

1. John Steinbeck
2. Floyd Dell
3. Eugene O'Neill
4. Eugene O'Neill
5. Wilkie Collins

95. First Person Possessive

1. Daphne du Maurier
2. Willa Cather
3. William Saroyan
4. Louis Nizer
5. Howard Spring

96. All Kinds of Men

1. *Under Western Skies*
2. *The Magic Mountain*
3. *1984*
4. *Pickwick Papers*
5. *Ulysses*

97. Peter, Peter

1. Henry James
2. Wallace Stevens
3. William Wordsworth
4. George du Maurier
5. Carl Van Vechten

98. Clothes Make the Man

1. Nicolai Gogol
2. Alberto Moravia
3. Sloan Wilson
4. Morris West
5. Michael Arlen

99. "Red"

1. O. Henry
2. Anatole France
3. Sean O'Casey
4. Dashiell Hammett
5. John Steinbeck

100. The Children's Corner

1. Mary Mapes Dodge
2. Lyman Frank Baum
3. Howard R. Garis
4. Gelett Burgess
5. Ludwig Bemelmans

101. The Four Seasons

1. *Spring's Awakening*
2. *The Winter of Our Discontent*
3. *Early Autumn*
4. *A Summer Place*
5. *After Many a Summer Dies the Swan*
6. *The Autumn Garden*
7. *The Torrents of Spring*
8. *A Winter's Tale*
9. *Black Spring*
10. *Summer and Smoke*

102. Trios

1. Roxane
2. Pantagruel
3. Ethan Frome
4. Adam Bede
5. Bathsheba Everdene

103. Siblings

1. Franny and Zooey
2. Dorothea and Celia Brooke
3. Miles and Flora
4. Roderick and Madeline Usher
5. Tom and Maggie Tulliver
6. Marianne and Elinor Dashwood
7. Holden and Phoebe Caulfield
8. Gretchen and Valentine
9. Hepzibah and Clifford Pyncheon
10. Sebastian and Viola

104. Children to the Fore

1. *The Innocent Voyage (A High Wind in Jamaica)*
2. *Lord of the Flies*
3. *Peter Grimes*
4. *Pied Piper of Hamelin*
5. *Pied Piper*

105. Same Titles, Different Authors

1. [A] Honoré de Balzac
   [B] William Saroyan
2. [A] Henry Wadsworth Longfellow
   [B] Lillian Hellman
3. [A] Thomas Paine
   [B] Jean-Paul Sartre
4. [A] John Donne
   [B] John Gunther

106. Place-names

1. *The Outcasts of Poker Flat*
2. *The Murders in the Rue Morgue*
3. *Appointment in Samarra*
4. *The Playboy of the Western World*
5. *Eyeless in Gaza*
6. *Christ Stopped at Eboli*
7. *Timon of Athens*
8. *Ruggles of Red Gap*
9. *Two Gentlemen of Verona*
10. "The Celebrated Jumping Frog of Calaveras County"

107. Astronomical

1. Lady Gregory
2. A. J. Cronin
3. Sean O'Casey
4. Jean Anouilh (Christopher Fry)
5. James T. Farrell

108. M.D.'s and Others

1. *Candide*
2. *Dr. Jekyll and Mr. Hyde*
3. Anton Chekhov, *Uncle Vanya*
4. *The Magnificent Obsession*
5. Boris Pasternak
6. *The Vicar of Wakefield*
7. *The Plague*
8. *The Citadel*
9. Molière, *Physician in Spite of Himself*
10. Mysteries of R. Austin Freeman

109. Trios

1. *Moby Dick*
2. *The Three Musketeers*
3. *Three Sisters*
4. *Desire Under the Elms*
5. *The Idiot*

110. Titular Locations

1. Evelyn Waugh
2. Erskine Caldwell
3. Maxwell Anderson
4. Sir James Barrie
5. John Hersey
6. Sarah Orne Jewett
7. Sir Walter Scott
8. Anthony Trollope
9. John Steinbeck
10. E. M. Forster

111. Mystery and Mysteries

1. Franz Cumont
2. Eugène Sue
3. Edgar Allan Poe
4. Mrs. Ann Radcliffe
5. Mark Twain

112. Theatre of War

1. World War I
2. Civil War
3. World War II
4. World War I
5. Napoleonic Wars

113. Behind the Mask

1. Saki
2. Emily Brontë
3. Voltaire
4. Washington Irving
5. Oscar Wilde
6. George Sand
7. George Orwell
8. Lewis Carroll
9. Stendhal
10. George Eliot

A CATALOGUE OF SELECTED DOVER BOOKS
IN ALL FIELDS OF INTEREST

A CATALOGUE OF SELECTED DOVER BOOKS
IN ALL FIELDS OF INTEREST

What Is Science?, *N. Campbell*
The role of experiment and measurement, the function of mathematics, the nature of scientific laws, the difference between laws and theories, the limitations of science, and many similarly provocative topics are treated clearly and without technicalities by an eminent scientist. "Still an excellent introduction to scientific philosophy," H. Margenau in *Physics Today.* "A first-rate primer . . . deserves a wide audience," *Scientific American.* 192pp. 5⅜ x 8.
60043-2 Paperbound $1.25

The Nature of Light and Colour in the Open Air, *M. Minnaert*
Why are shadows sometimes blue, sometimes green, or other colors depending on the light and surroundings? What causes mirages? Why do multiple suns and moons appear in the sky? Professor Minnaert explains these unusual phenomena and hundreds of others in simple, easy-to-understand terms based on optical laws and the properties of light and color. No mathematics is required but artists, scientists, students, and everyone fascinated by these "tricks" of nature will find thousands of useful and amazing pieces of information. Hundreds of observational experiments are suggested which require no special equipment. 200 illustrations; 42 photos. xvi + 362pp. 5⅜ x 8.
20196-1 Paperbound $2.00

The Strange Story of the Quantum, An Account for the General Reader of the Growth of Ideas Underlying Our Present Atomic Knowledge, *B. Hoffmann*
Presents lucidly and expertly, with barest amount of mathematics, the problems and theories which led to modern quantum physics. Dr. Hoffmann begins with the closing years of the 19th century, when certain trifling discrepancies were noticed, and with illuminating analogies and examples takes you through the brilliant concepts of Planck, Einstein, Pauli, Broglie, Bohr, Schroedinger, Heisenberg, Dirac, Sommerfeld, Feynman, etc. This edition includes a new, long postscript carrying the story through 1958. "Of the books attempting an account of the history and contents of our modern atomic physics which have come to my attention, this is the best," H. Margenau, Yale University, in *American Journal of Physics.* 32 tables and line illustrations. Index. 275pp. 5⅜ x 8.
20518-5 Paperbound $2.00

Great Ideas of Modern Mathematics: Their Nature and Use, *Jagjit Singh*
Reader with only high school math will understand main mathematical ideas of modern physics, astronomy, genetics, psychology, evolution, etc. better than many who use them as tools, but comprehend little of their basic structure. Author uses his wide knowledge of non-mathematical fields in brilliant exposition of differential equations, matrices, group theory, logic, statistics, problems of mathematical foundations, imaginary numbers, vectors, etc. Original publication. 2 appendixes. 2 indexes. 65 ills. 322pp. 5⅜ x 8.
20587-8 Paperbound $2.25

THE MUSIC OF THE SPHERES: THE MATERIAL UNIVERSE — FROM ATOM TO QUASAR, SIMPLY EXPLAINED, *Guy Murchie*
Vast compendium of fact, modern concept and theory, observed and calculated data, historical background guides intelligent layman through the material universe. Brilliant exposition of earth's construction, explanations for moon's craters, atmospheric components of Venus and Mars (with data from recent fly-by's), sun spots, sequences of star birth and death, neighboring galaxies, contributions of Galileo, Tycho Brahe, Kepler, etc.; and (Vol. 2) construction of the atom (describing newly discovered sigma and xi subatomic particles), theories of sound, color and light, space and time, including relativity theory, quantum theory, wave theory, probability theory, work of Newton, Maxwell, Faraday, Einstein, de Broglie, etc. "Best presentation yet offered to the intelligent general reader," *Saturday Review*. Revised (1967). Index. 319 illustrations by the author. Total of xx + 644pp. 5⅜ x 8½.
21809-0, 21810-4   Two volume set, paperbound $5.00

FOUR LECTURES ON RELATIVITY AND SPACE, *Charles Proteus Steinmetz*
Lecture series, given by great mathematician and electrical engineer, generally considered one of the best popular-level expositions of special and general relativity theories and related questions. Steinmetz translates complex mathematical reasoning into language accessible to laymen through analogy, example and comparison. Among topics covered are relativity of motion, location, time; of mass; acceleration; 4-dimensional time-space; geometry of the gravitational field; curvature and bending of space; non-Euclidean geometry. Index. 40 illustrations. x + 142pp. 5⅜ x 8½.   61771-8 Paperbound $1.35

HOW TO KNOW THE WILD FLOWERS, *Mrs. William Starr Dana*
Classic nature book that has introduced thousands to wonders of American wild flowers. Color-season principle of organization is easy to use, even by those with no botanical training, and the genial, refreshing discussions of history, folklore, uses of over 1,000 native and escape flowers, foliage plants are informative as well as fun to read. Over 170 full-page plates, collected from several editions, may be colored in to make permanent records of finds. Revised to conform with 1950 edition of Gray's Manual of Botany. xlii + 438pp. 5⅜ x 8½.   20332-8 Paperbound $2.50

MANUAL OF THE TREES OF NORTH AMERICA, *Charles Sprague Sargent*
Still unsurpassed as most comprehensive, reliable study of North American tree characteristics, precise locations and distribution. By dean of American dendrologists. Every tree native to U.S., Canada, Alaska; 185 genera, 717 species, described in detail—leaves, flowers, fruit, winterbuds, bark, wood, growth habits, etc. plus discussion of varieties and local variants, immaturity variations. Over 100 keys, including unusual 11-page analytical key to genera, aid in identification. 783 clear illustrations of flowers, fruit, leaves. An unmatched permanent reference work for all nature lovers. Second enlarged (1926) edition. Synopsis of families. Analytical key to genera. Glossary of technical terms. Index. 783 illustrations, 1 map. Total of 982pp. 5⅜ x 8.
20277-1, 20278-X Two volume set, paperbound $6.00

IT'S FUN TO MAKE THINGS FROM SCRAP MATERIALS,
Evelyn Glantz Hershoff
What use are empty spools, tin cans, bottle tops? What can be made from rubber bands, clothes pins, paper clips, and buttons? This book provides simply worded instructions and large diagrams showing you how to make cookie cutters, toy trucks, paper turkeys, Halloween masks, telephone sets, aprons, linoleum block- and spatter prints — in all 399 projects! Many are easy enough for young children to figure out for themselves; some challenging enough to entertain adults; all are remarkably ingenious ways to make things from materials that cost pennies or less! Formerly "Scrap Fun for Everyone." Index. 214 illustrations. 373pp. 5⅜ x 8½.   21251-3 Paperbound $1.75

SYMBOLIC LOGIC and THE GAME OF LOGIC, *Lewis Carroll*
"Symbolic Logic" is not concerned with modern symbolic logic, but is instead a collection of over 380 problems posed with charm and imagination, using the syllogism and a fascinating diagrammatic method of drawing conclusions. In "The Game of Logic" Carroll's whimsical imagination devises a logical game played with 2 diagrams and counters (included) to manipulate hundreds of tricky syllogisms. The final section, "Hit or Miss" is a lagniappe of 101 additional puzzles in the delightful Carroll manner. Until this reprint edition, both of these books were rarities costing up to $15 each. Symbolic Logic: Index. xxxi + 199pp. The Game of Logic: 96pp. 2 vols. bound as one. 5⅜ x 8.
20492-8 Paperbound $2.50

MATHEMATICAL PUZZLES OF SAM LOYD, PART I
selected and edited by M. Gardner
Choice puzzles by the greatest American puzzle creator and innovator. Selected from his famous collection, "Cyclopedia of Puzzles," they retain the unique style and historical flavor of the originals. There are posers based on arithmetic, algebra, probability, game theory, route tracing, topology, counter and sliding block, operations research, geometrical dissection. Includes the famous "14-15" puzzle which was a national craze, and his "Horse of a Different Color" which sold millions of copies. 117 of his most ingenious puzzles in all. 120 line drawings and diagrams. Solutions. Selected references. xx + 167pp. 5⅜ x 8.
20498-7 Paperbound $1.35

STRING FIGURES AND HOW TO MAKE THEM, *Caroline Furness Jayne*
107 string figures plus variations selected from the best primitive and modern examples developed by Navajo, Apache, pygmies of Africa, Eskimo, in Europe, Australia, China, etc. The most readily understandable, easy-to-follow book in English on perennially popular recreation. Crystal-clear exposition; step-by-step diagrams. Everyone from kindergarten children to adults looking for unusual diversion will be endlessly amused. Index. Bibliography. Introduction by A. C. Haddon. 17 full-page plates, 960 illustrations. xxiii + 401pp. 5⅜ x 8½.
20152-X Paperbound $2.25

PAPER FOLDING FOR BEGINNERS, *W. D. Murray and F. J. Rigney*
A delightful introduction to the varied and entertaining Japanese art of origami (paper folding), with a full, crystal-clear text that anticipates every difficulty; over 275 clearly labeled diagrams of all important stages in creation. You get results at each stage, since complex figures are logically developed from simpler ones. 43 different pieces are explained: sailboats, frogs, roosters, etc. 6 photographic plates. 279 diagrams. 95pp. 5⅝ x 8⅜.
20713-7 Paperbound $1.00

PRINCIPLES OF ART HISTORY,
H. Wölfflin
Analyzing such terms as "baroque," "classic," "neoclassic," "primitive," "picturesque," and 164 different works by artists like Botticelli, van Cleve, Dürer, Hobbema, Holbein, Hals, Rembrandt, Titian, Brueghel, Vermeer, and many others, the author establishes the classifications of art history and style on a firm, concrete basis. This classic of art criticism shows what really occurred between the 14th-century primitives and the sophistication of the 18th century in terms of basic attitudes and philosophies. "A remarkable lesson in the art of seeing," *Sat. Rev. of Literature.* Translated from the 7th German edition. 150 illustrations. 254pp. 6⅛ x 9¼. 20276-3 Paperbound $2.25

PRIMITIVE ART,
Franz Boas
This authoritative and exhaustive work by a great American anthropologist covers the entire gamut of primitive art. Pottery, leatherwork, metal work, stone work, wood, basketry, are treated in detail. Theories of primitive art, historical depth in art history, technical virtuosity, unconscious levels of patterning, symbolism, styles, literature, music, dance, etc. A must book for the interested layman, the anthropologist, artist, handicrafter (hundreds of unusual motifs), and the historian. Over 900 illustrations (50 ceramic vessels, 12 totem poles, etc.). 376pp. 5⅜ x 8.   20025-6 Paperbound $2.50

THE GENTLEMAN AND CABINET MAKER'S DIRECTOR,
Thomas Chippendale
A reprint of the 1762 catalogue of furniture designs that went on to influence generations of English and Colonial and Early Republic American furniture makers. The 200 plates, most of them full-page sized, show Chippendale's designs for French (Louis XV), Gothic, and Chinese-manner chairs, sofas, canopy and dome beds, cornices, chamber organs, cabinets, shaving tables, commodes, picture frames, frets, candle stands, chimney pieces, decorations, etc. The drawings are all elegant and highly detailed; many include construction diagrams and elevations. A supplement of 24 photographs shows surviving pieces of original and Chippendale-style pieces of furniture. Brief biography of Chippendale by N. I. Bienenstock, editor of *Furniture World.* Reproduced from the 1762 edition. 200 plates, plus 19 photographic plates. vi + 249pp. 9⅛ x 12¼.   21601-2 Paperbound $3.50

AMERICAN ANTIQUE FURNITURE: A BOOK FOR AMATEURS,
Edgar G. Miller, Jr.
Standard introduction and practical guide to identification of valuable American antique furniture. 2115 illustrations, mostly photographs taken by the author in 148 private homes, are arranged in chronological order in extensive chapters on chairs, sofas, chests, desks, bedsteads, mirrors, tables, clocks, and other articles. Focus is on furniture accessible to the collector, including simpler pieces and a larger than usual coverage of Empire style. Introductory chapters identify structural elements, characteristics of various styles, how to avoid fakes, etc. "We are frequently asked to name some book on American furniture that will meet the requirements of the novice collector, the beginning dealer, and . . . the general public. . . . We believe Mr. Miller's two volumes more completely satisfy this specification than any other work," *Antiques.* Appendix. Index. Total of vi + 1106pp. 7⅞ x 10¾. 21599-7, 21600-4 Two volume set, paperbound $7.50

THE BAD CHILD'S BOOK OF BEASTS, MORE BEASTS FOR WORSE CHILDREN, and A MORAL ALPHABET, *H. Belloc*
Hardly and anthology of humorous verse has appeared in the last 50 years without at least a couple of these famous nonsense verses. But one must see the entire volumes — with all the delightful original illustrations by Sir Basil Blackwood — to appreciate fully Belloc's charming and witty verses that play so subacidly on the platitudes of life and morals that beset his day — and ours. A great humor classic. Three books in one. Total of 157pp. 5⅜ x 8. •
20749-8 Paperbound $1.00

THE DEVIL'S DICTIONARY, *Ambrose Bierce*
Sardonic and irreverent barbs puncturing the pomposities and absurdities of American politics, business, religion, literature, and arts, by the country's greatest satirist in the classic tradition. Epigrammatic as Shaw, piercing as Swift, American as Mark Twain, Will Rogers, and Fred Allen, Bierce will always remain the favorite of a small coterie of enthusiasts, and of writers and speakers whom he supplies with "some of the most gorgeous witticisms of the English language" (H. L. Mencken). Over 1000 entries in alphabetical order. 144pp. 5⅜ x 8. 20487-1 Paperbound $1.00

THE COMPLETE NONSENSE OF EDWARD LEAR.
This is the only complete edition of this master of gentle madness available at a popular price. *A Book of Nonsense, Nonsense Songs, More Nonsense Songs and Stories* in their entirety with all the old favorites that have delighted children and adults for years. The Dong With A Luminous Nose, The Jumblies, The Owl and the Pussycat, and hundreds of other bits of wonderful nonsense. 214 limericks, 3 sets of Nonsense Botany, 5 Nonsense Alphabets, 546 drawings by Lear himself, and much more. 320pp. 5⅜ x 8. 20167-8 Paperbound $1.75

THE WIT AND HUMOR OF OSCAR WILDE, *ed. by Alvin Redman*
Wilde at his most brilliant, in 1000 epigrams exposing weaknesses and hypocrisies of "civilized" society. Divided into 49 categories—sin, wealth, women, America, etc.—to aid writers, speakers. Includes excerpts from his trials, books, plays, criticism. Formerly "The Epigrams of Oscar Wilde." Introduction by Vyvyan Holland, Wilde's only living son. Introductory essay by editor. 260pp. 5⅜ x 8. 20602-5 Paperbound $1.50

A CHILD'S PRIMER OF NATURAL HISTORY, *Oliver Herford*
Scarcely an anthology of whimsy and humor has appeared in the last 50 years without a contribution from Oliver Herford. Yet the works from which these examples are drawn have been almost impossible to obtain! Here at last are Herford's improbable definitions of a menagerie of familiar and weird animals, each verse illustrated by the author's own drawings. 24 drawings in 2 colors; 24 additional drawings. vii + 95pp. 6½ x 6. 21647-0 Paperbound $1.00

THE BROWNIES: THEIR BOOK, *Palmer Cox*
The book that made the Brownies a household word. Generations of readers have enjoyed the antics, predicaments and adventures of these jovial sprites, who emerge from the forest at night to play or to come to the aid of a deserving human. Delightful illustrations by the author decorate nearly every page. 24 short verse tales with 266 illustrations. 155pp. 6⅝ x 9¼.
21265-3 Paperbound $1.50

THE WONDERFUL WIZARD OF OZ, *L. F. Baum*
All the original W. W. Denslow illustrations in full color—as much a part of
"The Wizard" as Tenniel's drawings are of "Alice in Wonderland." "The
Wizard" is still America's best-loved fairy tale, in which, as the author expresses
it, "The wonderment and joy are retained and the heartaches and nightmares
left out." Now today's young readers can enjoy every word and wonderful picture of the original book. New introduction by Martin Gardner. A Baum
bibliography. 23 full-page color plates. viii + 268pp. 5⅜ x 8.
20691-2 Paperbound $1.95

THE MARVELOUS LAND OF OZ, *L. F. Baum*
This is the equally enchanting sequel to the "Wizard," continuing the adventures of the Scarecrow and the Tin Woodman. The hero this time is a little
boy named Tip, and all the delightful Oz magic is still present. This is the
Oz book with the Animated Saw-Horse, the Woggle-Bug, and Jack Pumpkin-
head. All the original John R. Neill illustrations, 10 in full color. 287pp.
5⅜ x 8.
20692-0 Paperbound $1.75

ALICE'S ADVENTURES UNDER GROUND, *Lewis Carroll*
The original *Alice in Wonderland*, hand-lettered and illustrated by Carroll
himself, and originally presented as a Christmas gift to a child-friend. Adults
as well as children will enjoy this charming volume, reproduced faithfully
in this Dover edition. While the story is essentially the same, there are slight
changes, and Carroll's spritely drawings present an intriguing alternative to
the famous Tenniel illustrations. One of the most popular books in Dover's
catalogue. Introduction by Martin Gardner. 38 illustrations. 128pp. 5⅜ x 8½.
21482-6 Paperbound $1.00

THE NURSERY "ALICE," *Lewis Carroll*
While most of us consider *Alice in Wonderland* a story for children of all
ages, Carroll himself felt it was beyond younger children. He therefore pro-
vided this simplified version, illustrated with the famous Tenniel drawings
enlarged and colored in delicate tints, for children aged "from Nought to
Five." Dover's edition of this now rare classic is a faithful copy of the 1889
printing, including 20 illustrations by Tenniel, and front and back covers
reproduced in full color. Introduction by Martin Gardner. xxiii + 67pp.
6⅛ x 9¼.
21610-1 Paperbound $1.75

THE STORY OF KING ARTHUR AND HIS KNIGHTS, *Howard Pyle*
A fast-paced, exciting retelling of the best known Arthurian legends for young
readers by one of America's best story tellers and illustrators. The sword
Excalibur, wooing of Guinevere, Merlin and his downfall, adventures of Sir
Pellias and Gawaine, and others. The pen and ink illustrations are vividly
imagined and wonderfully drawn. 41 illustrations. xviii + 313pp. 6⅛ x 9¼.
21445-1 Paperbound $2.00

Prices subject to change without notice.

Available at your book dealer or write for free catalogue to Dept. Adsci,
Dover Publications, Inc., 180 Varick St., N.Y., N.Y. 10014. Dover publishes more
than 150 books each year on science, elementary and advanced mathematics,
biology, music, art, literary history, social sciences and other areas.